Better

"Never trust a leader without a limp. The smooth paths produce smooth people. And smooth people break when things get hard. Andrew Horsfield has a limp. You can feel it in every page of this book. He is thoughtful, generous, and courageous, encouraging us to get uncomfortable in order to move forward. Andrew calls it the messy middle. The place where the old way meets the new way. It is a place of vulnerability and courage. Most people avoid it. This book takes you straight into it. It's a rare gift."

Cameron Schwab,
Design CEO

"A sharp, compassionate guide for anyone who's ever muttered 'How did my life get like... this?' *Better* slices through the stories that keep us small and offers practical, soul-level tools to get moving again. Equal parts tough love and genuine hope, this book is a wake-up call worth answering."

Jodi Wellman
Author of *You Only Die Once*

"Change is scary and burdensome when you have so much life to get through and the stakes are high. *Better* makes sense of fear and helped me identify the biggest roadblock to navigating challenge and change – me. This book makes doing the hard stuff easier. You'll come back to it often."

Gehan Davids
GM Financial Control, CFO Division, RACV

"A fulfilling life isn't run on default – it's designed. *Better* pulls you off autopilot and back into reflection, intentional momentum and renewed purpose. A quiet reset your mind will thank you for."

Marc Champagne
Best-selling author and Mental Fitness Strategist

"A deeply human and practical guide for navigating the high-pressure reality of modern leadership. Essential reading for anyone who wants to take control of their personal and professional life"

Phil Wells
Head of People Development & Learning, L'Oréal Groupe

"Andrew gives us something rare in this book. A set of simple, powerful practices that help us build the courage, capability and character to step beyond the status quo and live with more passion and purpose. A fantastic read."

Mykel Dixon
Award winning speaker and author of *Everyday Creative*

"This book will support and inspire you to take up the challenge to be better. A journey of self-discovery, you will understand yourself, the value of struggle, and how to align your aspirations and actions to improve every area of your life."

Lisa Alexander AM
High Performance Coach and former
Australian Diamonds Head Coach

"I'm often engaged by businesses to discuss leadership and what makes an elite team. Unfortunately, many are looking for a magic wand. Andrew understands that mastery is made up of millions of little moments, and in this book, shines a light on the practices you need to pursue your own form of mastery."

Nick Maxwell
CEO of Eclat Corporation and former
Collingwood Football Club captain

Escape average.
Beat burnout.
Own your life.

Better

Andrew Horsfield

Published by Andrew Horsfield 2026

Book design and typesetting:
Duncan Blachford, Typography Studio

978-1-7644925-0-8 (paperback)

Catalogue records for this book are available from the National Library of Australia.

Printed by Griffin Press

andrewhorsfield.com

To Sarah, Ben and Isabelle, of course

Contents

"Success isn't a magic list nobody knows, it's an obvious list nobody does"

ALEX HORMOZI

Introduction

Roger Federer was born in Basel, Switzerland, in 1981. He was drawn to many sports as a child, but most of all to tennis. He was a prodigy, a natural, and by his late teens he was a professional player known for his elegant, almost balletic style. Over the next two decades, he would win twenty Grand Slam titles, including a record eight at Wimbledon. He was ranked number one in the world for 310 weeks. His play was so graceful, so seemingly without strain, that it was often described with a single word: effortless. Federer's trajectory is the stuff of fairy tales: natural talent combined with graceful execution that culminated in towering success.

The problem with this account of Federer's career path is that it ignores the years of struggle. Like many athletes, Federer struggled for years before he broke through. He was known for his emotional outbursts, whining, swearing and regular racket-throwing. His parents, coaches and even his rivals questioned his ability to win tough matches. Early in his career, an opponent at the Italian Open publicly questioned his mental discipline, saying, 'Roger will be the favourite for the first two hours, and then I'll be the favourite after that.'

The truth, as Federer would later admit, was that he had to work very hard to navigate that point of his career – and eventually make success look easy. What makes Roger Federer different from many other champions who have experienced success is his openness around how much he struggled early in his career.

On 9 June 2024 Federer delivered the commencement address at Dartmouth College. His speech reflected his two decades of dedication. He talked about the days when he felt broken, when his back hurt, his knee hurt, when he was sick or scared, but still had to find a way to win. He talked about the years of training when nobody was watching, the endless work to master his emotions and his game.

And he cited a surprising statistic rarely associated with his success: in the 1526 singles matches he played in his career, while he won almost 80 per cent of the time, he only won 54 per cent of the points he played. He spent nearly half his career losing. 'When you lose every second point, on average,' he explained, 'you learn not to dwell on every shot. To succeed you must become a master at overcoming hard moments. To me, that is the sign of a champion.'

Federer is the embodiment of tennis success. He has the awards, the fame, the money, the critical acclaim and the records. But by his account he was losing almost half the time. His speech attracted millions of views and inspired dozens of media pieces. It became notable because it was unusual for a champion to reveal the wrinkles beneath a journey that from afar appeared unblemished.

Getting stuck isn't something champions routinely discuss in agonising detail, so when our own lives get a little messy and bumpy we can feel isolated and alone. The aim of this book is to help you realise that the struggles you face are not a sign that things are wrong; they are a signal you are striving for something right.

A practice to master

We see the effortless grace of a champion like Roger Federer and assume it's a gift, but his commencement speech reinforces a different story. The most influential part of his career, and most critical factor for his success, was his ability to navigate the messy middle. Being able to consistently overcome challenge, setback and struggle. This is difficult for most of us to do because we have been conditioned to see struggle as a problem. Our culture is obsessed with beginnings and endings. The exciting launch of a new venture or the triumphant crossing of a finish line.

We love stories of overnight success and dramatic transformations. But we rarely talk about the difficulties we face in moving through the messy middle.

Whether you're building a career, rebuilding a relationship or rebuilding yourself, improvement requires you to move through the messy middle. And while every messy middle is unique to the person working through it, messy middles are always challenging because we have to put ourselves on the hook in order to move from where we are to where we want to be.

Sadly, rather than accept this responsibility, many of us are choosing to step back and settle. We know we have plateaued, but struggle to find a way forward, and despite feeling trapped, choose to keep going. Applying the practices in this book will help you navigate what's keeping you stuck, so you can advance your personal and professional life.

But why should you bother? Why should you willingly step into this challenging space? Why choose to engage with the mess when it would be so much easier to stay on the sidelines where it's safe and comfortable?

Because everything you want in life is on the other side of it. The fulfilling career that uses your talents and makes a meaningful impact? It exists in the difficulty of learning new skills, taking on projects that stretch you, speaking up when you have a different point of view, and perhaps even making a leap into a new role or industry. It's not handed to you. It's earned through the courage to move beyond your comfort zone.

That sense of vitality and energy you want? It's on the other side of early morning workouts you don't feel like doing, the discipline to choose nourishing food over convenient junk, and the patience to keep going when the scale doesn't move for a week. The messiness isn't a problem to solve, it's a practice to master.

We are wired to seek comfort and avoid difficulty. But a life lived entirely in comfort is a small life. Embracing the messy middle is your antidote to average. It's deciding to trade the illusion of safety for the reality of your own strength, and living a life of meaning, growth and purpose. And building assets along the way like resilience, wisdom, self-respect and the quiet, unshakeable confidence that comes from knowing you can handle hard things. Realising that struggle is not an obstacle to the life you want. It's lighting the path to get you there.

No secrets or simple path

This is not a book of abstract theories or simplistic five-step formulas. The messy middle by its nature is complex, so a five-step formula or simple set of life hacks isn't going to help you. You need a guide that equips you with a suite of practical and adaptable skills you can use in the real world, under real pressure.

This book is structured around the Better Life Index™ which is made up of three core attributes – character, capability and courage. Each attribute has a corresponding question that will help direct you to the practice that will be most helpful when you feel like you have lost your way:

1. Who am I? (Character)
2. What am I capable of? (Capability)
3. What's getting in the way? (Courage)

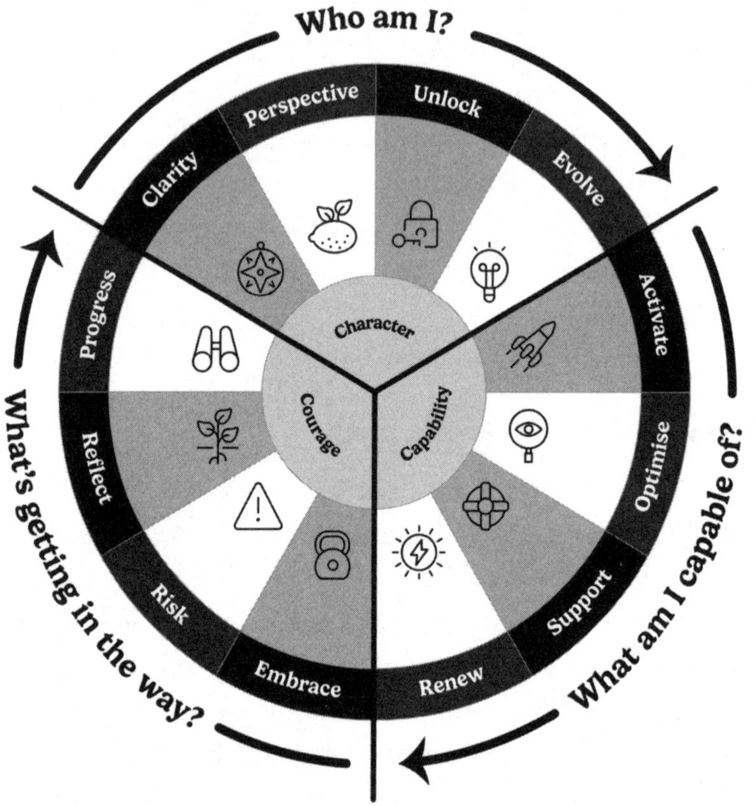

It's easy to dismiss these three simple questions or think they cannot possibly be adequate to help you manage the messiness of life – and that's okay. It's natural in moments of uncertainty to try to reduce your feelings of fear and anxiety, by rushing towards a quick fix or neatly packaged outcome.

But there is another way.

You can turn uncertainty into your teacher.

The forces holding us back can sometimes be hard to see. Great questions expose these forces, opening up valuable insights that, when acted upon, can lead you to the better life you are seeking. The practices in this book are intended to create a positive shift in your perspective, because the circumstances that keep us stuck are largely created by the narrative we carry with us. When we change the narrative around those circumstances, our world view begins to change, and new opportunities emerge.

Personal transformation becomes possible.

You just need to make a start.

So jump in and find out more about the various practices you can build to develop greater character, capability and courage. The insights and prompts in each chapter will help you apply each practice to your own life circumstance. The Better Life Index™ is not a tool for a certain type of person, at a specific point in their career, or someone with specific career aspirations. They are a suite of practices designed to help you re-imagine your life; however you choose to define that goal.

The turning point

What happens when you get good at this? What's the benefit of learning to master the messy middle? The change is profound, and it goes far beyond simply achieving your goals more effectively. It changes how you experience your life.

First, you gain a deep and resilient sense of agency. You move from feeling like a victim of your circumstances to being the author of your responses. You understand that while you can't control everything that happens to you, you always have a choice in how you engage with it. This shift is the foundation of all personal power. The feeling of being stuck dissolves, replaced by the quiet confidence that you can always find a productive next step. The world stops happening to you, and you start happening to the world.

Second, you find a new kind of freedom. It's not freedom from responsibility; it's the freedom that comes with capability. The freedom to be ambitious without being terrified of the struggle. The freedom to pursue big, interesting and scary goals, because you know you have the tools to handle the inevitable messiness that comes with them. No longer being held captive by the fear of what might go wrong, because you have trust in your ability to handle whatever comes your way. Freeing you up to live a bigger, more expansive life.

Third, you develop a sustainable way to perform. You learn how to operate at a high level without burning yourself out. You understand that managing your energy is just as important as managing your time and learn to build practices of renewal and reflection into your life. You stop seeing rest as a weakness and start seeing it as a critical component to achieving the results you seek. You move from a model of frantic, unsustainable sprinting to one of a strong, steady and powerful pace that you can maintain for the long haul.

Ultimately, learning to navigate the messy middle allows you to live a life that is aligned with your values and full of purpose. You close the gap between the person you are and the person you want to be. You stop living a life that just looks good and start living one that feels good. You build a career, relationships and a sense of self that are not only successful, but deeply fulfilling.

The act of working to make your life better isn't easy. It requires honesty, effort and a willingness to be uncomfortable. But the reward is a life lived with more enjoyment, satisfaction and purpose. It's the path to becoming not just a better leader, parent or professional, but a better you.

The work is challenging, but it's worth it.

You just need to start.

Character

Life doesn't build character, it reveals it.

STEVIE WONDER

Most of us know we are unlikely to die on a rollercoaster. Statistically, it's far more dangerous to drive to the amusement park than get on the ride. Yet despite knowing it's safe, a good rollercoaster terrifies us from the first climb to the jarring stop at the end. It's *designed* that way. The twists, turns, noise and speed override our rational brain and activate the amygdala, the prehistoric part of our brain hardwired to avoid danger.

The part that *thinks* the ride is scary.

Our modern life is full of rollercoasters.

The job interview is an employment rollercoaster, with interviewers asking questions that incite panic for some applicants (but possibility for the rest). The school pick-up is a different kind of rollercoaster. One where parents worry about social hierarchy or whether they're sending their child to the right swim school. Ending a relationship is a relentless rollercoaster of grief and relief as you question whether you made the right decision.

The biggest rollercoaster of them all is the messy middle. The frightening space we must navigate to get from where we are to where we want to be. A space that holds opportunity but also, even more powerfully, the perception that you are one misstep away from being fired, ostracised, missing your big break or exposed as the fraud you think you are.

Of course usually none of this is true, but your amygdala doesn't know that. Just like it doesn't know that riding on a rollercoaster won't kill you.

Which is why character is so crucial.

One part of us wants to ride the rollercoaster. We want to improve our life, make time for what matters and have a personal and professional impact. Another, more primitive, part of us wants to play it safe. When we choose safety, we passively accept the status quo as our lot in life. We build elaborate stories and alibis to justify our choice, and if we listen to them for long enough can forget we even had a choice or that we are allowed to change.

Boarding the rollercoaster builds character.

We develop the mental and moral skills that help us navigate the change we are trying to make. Skills that enable us to be bold, and which may have been lying dormant until now. These skills allow us to own who we are and what we believe in and express this fully in our lives. Finding yourself firmly wedged in the messy middle isn't an obstacle, it's an opportunity. The messy middle is the thick jungle designed to keep people away from the hidden treasure.

My friend Garry was a professional athlete who transitioned successfully into a career after sport. Like many people, during the Covid pandemic he was forced to reinvent his role as a keynote speaker. We brainstormed for a few hours, and I shared some approaches he could use to set up at home, present his keynotes online and maintain his business by serving clients who wanted to hire him.

Then he said, 'That's way out of my comfort zone, Andrew.'

There it was. The messy middle sitting right in front of us.

Garry didn't want the industry to change dramatically, but it did. I shared all the ways he had already explored things inside his comfort zone, and why he needed to make a change. In a difficult time, and in an already competitive industry, he needed to stretch himself and how he engaged with his market. Garry was visibly uncomfortable, scared and stuck.

Luckily, Garry had loads of character.

You need character most when you feel stuck.

Like when you are attempting something difficult and feel outmatched, overwhelmed or out of ideas. When you are experiencing the same recurring problem or pattern of behaviour and are uncertain about how to progress. Or when you experience a crisis of confidence and see the best in everyone else but the worst in yourself. These are not the times for gushing optimism or denying something difficult is happening. They are the times you must accept reality and look for the possibilities within the problem. Or, at the very least, take whatever benefit you can to steal the good fortune from misfortune.

It's a simple idea, but hardly a small one.

If this book was titled *How to Stay the Same*, we wouldn't need to address character. But it's not. It's titled *Better*, which means riding some rollercoasters that may be uncertain, risky and scary. Which is fine. We all get scared. That's the price we must pay if we choose to change our life for the better.

Most people won't pay that price.

Don't be most people.

Choose character.

1

Clarity

Pursue what matters.

Jennifer appears to have it all. A respected leader in her organisation, Jen has built an impressive career and forged a strong reputation. Being in a senior role she receives a significant salary, and constantly praises and promotes members of her team as the reason for her success. She is proud of the work she does but knows nothing would get done without the dedication and drive of her team. Her love for her work and her team makes her a magnet for talent.

Alongside her work, Jen is raising two kids, exercises five to six times a week, and has a monthly catch-up with her girlfriends. From the outside, her life is a success story. A highlight reel of accolades and achievements. People admire who she is and how she works, and actively seek her advice and want to spend time in her company.

I've been Jen's performance coach for years. In that time we have covered a variety of deeply personal issues, which come with deeply personal emotions. So when Jen started to become frustrated and emotional in one of our coaching sessions, there was no need for panic. I just gave her some time, slid the tissues across the table, and asked, 'Tell me, Jen, what's going on?'

'It's silly really, I don't know why I'm so upset. I've just got a lot on right now. The new project is taking longer than we thought and I'm the one holding up the launch. No matter how hard I work there is always more to do, and I'm just not getting back to people. They call and follow up but that just makes me feel bad, as I'm constantly apologising for not having got back to them sooner. The work is constant, the kids aren't sleeping very well and I feel tired all the time. Adrian and I try and share the load pretty evenly, but my life just feels like an endless slog right now.

'Don't get me wrong. I love what I'm doing, and I'm across most of the important stuff, but I feel constantly under siege. If it's not work, it's the housework, washing, running kids to sport on the weekend and then back to work for more of the same. I'm just so tired.'

There are a lot of people just like Jen.

You might be one of them.

Outwardly successful, doing good things, but most of your days are a blur of motion without much meaning. You wake up, reach for your phone and let the urgency of life take over before you've even had time to eat breakfast. Your mornings are a rush, and your calendar is a back-to-back Tetris game of other people's priorities. You are busy, really busy, and pushing through obstacles, but your days aren't counting, they're just accumulating.

Deep down you know you're destined for more but you feel imprisoned by the pressures of life. You're not unhappy, there's just a quiet hum of discontent beneath the surface of your busy, successful life. You're stuck in the uncomfortable space between the life you have and the one you want. You can feel the gap. You just don't know how to close it.

Improving what *isn't* working is relatively easy. Improving what is working can be completely terrifying.

You are successfully stuck.

Chasing happiness

If you pay attention to people and conversations, you quickly learn that most people operate under a deeply held assumption conveyed to them by their parents, schools, workplaces and society: that happiness is waiting for us at the finish line. If you work hard, you will become successful, and when you become successful, you'll be happy.

When I buy the house, *then* I'll feel secure.

When I lose the weight, *then* I'll feel confident.

When I find the relationship, *then* I'll feel complete.

But here's what actually happens.

You work hard towards your goal. You sacrifice, strategise, push through obstacles and, eventually, cross the finish line. For a brief, glorious moment, you feel exactly the way you thought you would. Validated. Successful. Like you have arrived. And then, almost imperceptibly, that feeling begins to fade. The destination doesn't deliver what you thought it would.

In no time at all, that achievement you thought would change everything becomes your new normal. The promotion becomes just your job. The house becomes just where you live. The weight loss becomes just how you look.

The goalposts shift. So you set a new finish line. And start the cycle all over again. Chasing a feeling of lasting satisfaction that never quite arrives as you push aside the things that really matter to you to pursue a narrower version of what success looks like and how it is measured. You work long hours and keep a relentless schedule that serves other people, irrespective of the personal cost, wondering why contentment seems so elusive.

You are busy but not fulfilled.

Productive, but rarely purposeful.

Living a life that doesn't feel like your own.

This might be the reason you feel stuck. You are perpetually dissatisfied with the present because you are chasing an imagined future that never arrives. Ignoring that success, and lifelong happiness, comes from navigating the messy present, not chasing some future finish line.

When you align the decisions you make, the actions you take and the outcomes you serve, happiness becomes possible.

You won't be immune to the setbacks and struggle that comes with striving for something worthwhile, but you will experience greater levels of health, happiness and success.

If you feel like you have lost your way, now is the time to crawl out from the expectations and external pressures you are under and reclaim your life.

Living on purpose

Alfred Nobel was a Swedish chemist, engineer and successful businessman who held 355 patents during his lifetime, including his most famous invention, dynamite. Alfred, along with his brother Ludvig, purchased a steel mill in 1894, and using his strong aptitude for science and chemistry developed the business to become a major armament manufacturer.

One morning in 1888 Alfred opened his morning newspaper to find his own obituary. The headline read: 'The Merchant of Death Is Dead!' The article describing him as the man who 'became rich by finding ways to kill more people faster than ever before'. There was just one problem. Alfred wasn't dead. His brother Ludvig had died, and the newspaper had mixed them up.

Reading his own obituary was a wake-up call.

Alfred was horrified that this was how the world saw him, and his work. Not because the obituary was wrong about his death, but because it was right about his life.

He had become successful by society's standards while losing sight of what actually mattered to him. This insight led

Alfred to make a decision that would change everything. He set aside the bulk of his estate to establish the Nobel Prizes, awards given to people who contribute 'the greatest benefit to mankind'. This is how we remember Alfred Nobel today.

At the heart of the practice I describe in this book is addressing the gap between your current life and the life you want to be living: just like Alfred Nobel did. It's not always easy and may require you to make choices that disappoint others. But this is the path to living a life that is authentically yours.

Sceptics criticise Alfred, suggesting his motive for creating the prize was to improve his reputation. However, unbeknown to his critics and family, he had already established a trust dedicating a proportion of his wealth to the development and achievement of science. The early obituary notice merely accelerated the timing of his contribution.

You don't have to wait until you are declared dead to start living a life that matters. Nor would I suggest you start by defining your values, writing a personal mission statement or deciding on the legacy you want to leave. While these can be valuable, they are too abstract, too hard and take too long, so rarely get done.

Meaning is rare, but it's not mystical. It's not reserved for monks or philosophers or people who have figured out a grand purpose for their life. It's found by cultivating three qualities that research has proven dramatically improves the quality of our life:

Coherence. Your life makes sense to you. You make choices that enable your actions to tell a consistent story about who you are. When you choose to listen to a frustrated colleague, you're not just solving a problem, you're being the leader you want to be. When you put your phone away during dinner, you're not just avoiding distraction, you're choosing to be a present parent. Your life stops being a series of random events and starts feeling like a unified whole.

Purpose. You have goals and direction. You consciously manage your time, energy and attention, because you value the difference between general motion and moving towards something that matters. It's recognising you need to work late to achieve a specific goal, not just serve a default habit. Purpose is what turns your to-do list and obligations into a more discerning set of intentional choices that serve a specific goal. You choose to live intentionally, not accidentally.

Mattering. Your presence has a positive impact. You have a quiet confidence that makes a difference to the people and projects around you. And you act not to seek applause or recognition but to make a valuable contribution. When you leave a conversation, people feel heard. When the project succeeds, you are the first to give praise. When the traffic is congested, you allow someone to merge. You are consistently making things better.

These qualities are not abstract ideals or something you have to spend months trying to work out. They are created as a direct result of living with intention. Which, as it happens, will not only help you achieve what matters to you, it will also teach you something far more important: to trust yourself. To follow your instincts and let your heart have a lot more input on your decisions and actions. You will not be immune to the messiness of life but will navigate it more effectively and experience a deeper level of satisfaction at the end of the day, because you are living on purpose.

Transition with intention

Over the two decades of my career, I've found the most effective way to help people live more intentionally is to simply highlight the power of purposeful transitions.

What do I mean by transitions? Well, every morning when you wake up and start your day, you engage in a transition from rest to activation. When you drop your kids to school and start your commute to work, you transition from family time to travel time. When you end your commute and arrive home, you are making a transition from professional time to personal time.

Our days are made up of a series of these transitions.

Each of these transitions gives you the opportunity to show up in a way aligned with how you want to live your life. I'm convinced that if you choose to be more mindful about how you shift from one activity to the next, you can revitalise your life. Over the next week, as you move from one activity to another during your day, try this three-step exercise:

1. Calm your mind

Give yourself two minutes to quieten your brain and find a sense of calm. This doesn't have to be complicated. You don't need to sit down or find a quiet space to meditate. You're simply trying to create a pause to relax your body and turn down the chatter in your mind. You may find this hard to do at first, but don't worry. The aim is simply to create a moment of stillness between what you were doing and what you're about to do in the time that's available to you.

This step matters because when your mind is racing, your nervous system is activated and you carry tension from one activity to the next. You are rushing and reactive, not calm and composed. Taking time to calm your mind creates the space for you to live with intentionality.

2. Clarify your intention

This is the powerful step that helps you shift from autopilot to awareness. Most of us lead busy lives and move from one thing to the next without ever asking how we want to show up. But these transitions are the moments that determine how consistently we integrate coherence, purpose and mattering into our life. Ask yourself three questions to clarify your intentions:

What role am I playing? We all have different roles we play in life. We are leaders, parents, coaches, contributors and friends. Being clear about the role you're fulfilling in each moment anchors you in who you need to be at that point in time. You're not the same person in every context. The role you play as a parent is different from the role you play as a professional. When you're clear about your role, you can show up with clarity instead of confusion.

What reputation do I want? Your reputation enters a room long before you do. This isn't just what people think of you, it's the energy and presence you bring into any space you enter. Helpful. Calm. Impactful. Fun. When you are conscious about your reputation, you are more likely to make choices that align with who you want to be, not just what you want to accomplish. Which helps reduce incongruencies between what you say and what you do.

What result am I trying to achieve? Not every interaction needs to produce a tangible outcome, but every interaction has a purpose. Maybe it's connection. Maybe it's progress on a project. Maybe it's simply being present with someone you love. The foundation for making good choices is knowing the outcome you want from the situation you are in. Asking, 'What energy do I want to bring to this activity?' or 'What would a great outcome look like?' are helpful prompts that ensure you are present and purposeful. When you're clear about the result, you can prioritise what matters and let go of what doesn't.

3. Commit to action

Having completed the previous steps, your mind should now be primed for action. This is where the process becomes most valuable. Intentions are good, but actions are better. If your intention is to be more present with your kids, then turn off your phone as soon as you get home. If your intention is to be more collaborative in a meeting, then make fewer statements and ask more questions. If your intention is to be calm under pressure, then take a few deep breaths before responding to a difficult email. These small actions, made consciously again and again, compound into significant change, building a life of coherence, purpose and significance.

Life is a series of small transitions.

Far too often, we fail to make these transitions successfully.

I've seen coaches whose teams are behind on the scoreboard carry stress into their half-time address. I've seen leaders bring their bad day home to their family. I've seen team meetings erupt because emotions are frayed. And I've seen presentations implode because the presenter became a victim to their nerves before they even entered the room.

Building a deliberate practice to transition with intention enables you to connect with what gives your life meaning and make conscious decisions aligned to who you are and how you want to live. Give it a go. It's a remarkably powerful practice.

Compelling, not conforming

You are only on this planet for a limited time. It makes sense to spend that time wisely and in service of something personally meaningful.

You can be the author of your own life, or you can be passive. You can react to your circumstances, or you can create the conditions that give your life energy and spark. You can fit in with others or follow your own path. You can give away your freedom or embrace the power of personal agency.

The choice is yours.

It doesn't matter whether you step, stride or leap, but living with intention is the fastest path from where you are to where you want to be. To live a life that is compelling rather than conforming. You will probably feel unsteady at first, but your intuition and confidence will strengthen, deepen and grow, enabling you to create space and see opportunities you would have otherwise overlooked.

Life is short.

Make yours meaningful.

Insight ⤻ Action

Premise

We chase finish lines, believing happiness waits there. But the moment we arrive, the feeling fades. The achievement becomes our new normal. We are busy, living at a frenetic pace, but feeling less and less fulfilled.

Practice

This week, as you transition from one activity to another, pause for two minutes. Calm your mind. Then ask yourself three things: What role am I playing right now? What reputation do I want to bring to this space? What result am I trying to create? Than commit to one action that aligns with your intention. Not a grand gesture. Just one thing that makes your life feel more like yours.

Promise

You will immediately start to feel the difference between being busy and building a life that feels calm and coherent. You will gain more energy and realise living on purpose isn't mystical, it's just a series of intentional choices.

2

Perspective

Frame your experience

In the movie *Evan Almighty*, Steve Carell plays Evan Baxter, a congressional candidate who wants to change the world. The night before the elections, Evan prays to God asking that he grant him a successful election result. His wife Joan prays too, asking that she, Evan and their three sons might somehow find a way to become closer as a family.

After winning the election, Evan is shocked when God pays him a visit and throws him a challenge of Biblical proportions. The Lord wants him to build an ark and line up animals two-by-two in preparation for the flood. Despite initially avoiding God's request, Evan soon starts looking more and more like Noah and is followed by a pair of animals wherever he goes. It doesn't take long for Evan's appearance and growing commitment to build the ark to start to take a toll on the family. Neighbours gossip over hedges and the kids are bullied at school; the family is pushed further and further apart.

There is a brilliant scene in the movie where Joan is having dinner in the local diner. God, taking her order disguised as a waiter, asks, 'Are you okay?' She sits and stares at him, then confesses to the complete stranger that her husband has been making headlines for all the wrong reasons, as the 'New York Noah'. The media is having a field day and she is caught in the middle, trying to figure out if her husband has lost his mind.

'My husband says God told him to do it,' she says, her voice carrying that particular exhaustion that comes from explaining the unexplainable one too many times. 'What do you do with that?'

After listening thoughtfully, the waiter says, 'Sounds like an opportunity.' But Joan's not looking for feel-good platitudes. She needs real answers to a real problem. She pushes back, wanting more.

'Let me ask you something,' he says. 'If someone prays for patience, do you think God gives them patience? Or does he give them the opportunity to be patient? If they prayed for courage, does God give them courage or the chance to be courageous? If someone, let's say, prayed for their family to be closer, do you think God zaps them with warm fuzzy feelings or does He give them opportunities to love each other?'

And that's when the penny drops.

Joan understands the meaning of her messiness.

She was expecting divine intervention to deliver her a solution like room service. Ordered up, delivered promptly and looking exactly like she had imagined. But that's the thing about opportunities. They rarely arrive with clear instructions or comfortable timelines. They show up looking like problems that need solving, challenges that need facing or relationships that need more work than we thought we signed up for. This is where most of us get stuck.

We miss the fundamental truth about how growth, love and transformation work in the real world. They don't arrive as feelings or circumstances that make life easier. They arrive like nothing you expected – but everything you have needed. Invitations to become someone who can handle whatever life brings.

Life rarely goes to plan

Our lives rarely unfold according to plan. Ark building dilemmas are rare, but during our daily lives we all face situations that can feel overwhelming, impossible and just plain inconvenient. Do any of these sound familiar?

The mundane meeting. It appears on your calendar as a routine meeting, but as soon as it starts the agenda dissolves. The conversation meanders from one unrelated topic to another – and what began as a 'quick check-in' has slowly transformed into an hour-long conversation fest. Nothing gets solved, but everyone leaves frustrated with even more action items than before.

The assembly project. It looked doable in the store. A simple bookshelf with a few basic parts. But now your living room floor is covered in screws, wooden pegs and an instruction manual with nothing more than a few pictures to guide you. What was supposed to be a quick, satisfying task has morphed into a two-hour puzzle that tests your patience, your logic and your will to live.

The unexpected diagnosis. It was a routine check-up. You arrived expecting a clean bill of health, but the doctor's expression shifts, her tone of voice changes and you instantly feel the weight of their words. Your entire world shifts on its axis. Your stable, predictable rhythm of life evaporates, replaced by a fog of uncertainty. A gnawing fear of the unknown follows you out of the clinic and into a world that now looks terrifyingly fragile.

You can't always see these events coming, but since you have more control over them than you think, you can often turn them into something. The problem for most of us is that we tend not to live our lives this way. When we feel frustrated, restricted or stuck, we routinely place the blame squarely on other people or circumstances. Fault is rarely ours. It's usually someone else's.

There is good in most things if we are prepared to look for it. We are just bad at looking, often closing our eyes to the opportunity we have being given. Your emotions may tell you something is negative, unfair or unfavourable, but that doesn't mean you have to agree. You don't have to fall into negative thinking patterns that trap you in emotional turmoil. You can use perspective. You can separate the event that happens and the perspective you decide to view it through; and the right perspective can cut any obstacle down to size.

Most people can identify the unhelpful feelings that come with unexpected or unfavourable events in our lives. What separates those who feel unflappable is their ability to control their emotions and see things objectively. They focus their attention not on the problem but on the possibility within it.

Every obstacle you face, every dilemma, potential opportunity or problem you confront, exists within a particular frame or point of view. When you train your brain to find the most helpful point of view, you begin to see the possibilities within it. You become aware of the numerous paths you can take to solve the problem or dilemma, reach your potential and live a good life.

Finding perspective in an unfavourable situation you are facing isn't always fun, but it can be done. It's just a matter of whether we are willing to do so.

Problems into possibilities

George Clooney spent his early years in Hollywood getting rejected. He would approach an audition believing that if the producer and director liked him, he would get the role. He spent more time building rapport than showcasing his skill, so regularly missed out on roles. The constant knockbacks took their toll. He became discouraged and blamed the system for his lack of success.

This is something we are all guilty of doing at times: blaming the things beyond our control for our struggle or stress. Not realising that whining, though it may feel good, fails to move us forward in any significant way. When whining becomes a habit, we lose our perspective, power and personal agency. Something Clooney eventually realised, which changed everything.

Instead of arriving at the auditions thinking, 'I'm a desperate out-of-work actor who needs people to like me to give me a chance', Clooney decided to reframe the audition experience as an opportunity to display his skills and show the producer and director he was the solution to their problem. 'They have a role to fill, and I can show them I'm exactly what they are looking for.' This shift in perspective completely changed his energy, preparation and presence. Having deeply considered what the casting director needed for the role, he was able not only to showcase his acting ability but to project confidence that he was the right man for the role.

This is the power of perspective in action. The same person, with the same skills, performing in the same audition room, achieving an entirely different outcome because of how he chose to frame his experience. Choosing to become the solution to a problem rather than a problem seeking a solution.

This is the challenge for all of us, especially when we find ourselves stuck: to develop a mental framework that expands rather than restricts what we perceive to be possible. Every situation comes with an opportunity for action – and actions that move us forward are often the antidote to our predicament.

Of all the strategies we are going to talk about in this book, this is the most important. This is the one that gives your life the most leverage.

When people underestimate you, you can choose to prove them wrong. When people are argumentative, you can choose to create a deeper connection. When another request arrives in your overflowing inbox, you can choose what gets your time and attention.

Problems that get put under pressure ultimately break apart. They have no choice. As soon as you decide to tackle them, work around them or make them irrelevant, there is little left for them to resist.

By reframing obstacles as opportunities, you navigate the messy middle more effectively because you become more resourceful, more resilient and more capable. This is how perspective becomes the currency for a better life.

Mental flexibility

Finding perspective is primarily about mental flexibility. The willingness to question assumptions and look at the situations where we feel stuck from a fresh perspective. Being prepared to not see only what is present but seek out what might also be conspicuously absent.

But how do you do that?

Stories about movies and celebrities are entertaining, but what does this look like on a Sunday night when you feel fatigued and don't want to go back to work? What does it look like when you're dealing with a personal dilemma? Or when you need to move on after an argument? How do you actually find perspective? Here are five useful methods for getting started.

1. Reframe your experience

We get down on ourselves in the depth of struggle. We get disappointed and discouraged and form a negative view of the world, and sometimes of ourselves. Giving ourselves care and compassion is a great antidote for self-loathing. Challenge and a sense of struggle often signal that we are moving beyond what's obvious, comfortable or been done before. And the best results rarely come easily. Reframing productive struggle as a normal part of the human experience can alter our perspective and propel us forward.

2. Ask powerful questions

Overlooking our own contribution to the struggle we are in is a trap we can all fall into. Like whining about being busy and overwhelmed while ignoring our inability to say 'no'. Telling yourself 'My boss is unreasonable' is not particularly helpful or useful. It's just a negative statement. Asking a powerful question like 'How might I have a better relationship with my boss?' detangles emotions, releases your mind and reorients the conversation. Frustration is released, ideas start to flow and new possibilities can be explored.

3. Embrace your curiosity

Teachers will speak softly to calm a classroom full of noisy kids. Making it harder to hear forces students to be quieter so they can hear what's happening. We sometimes need to do the same. We become less curious as we get older, making it harder for us to find escape routes when we feel stuck. Forcing ourselves to consider alternate perspectives (without having to agree with them) helps assumptions to surface and we can then determine if the position we are taking best serves the outcome we are seeking.

4. Live your values

Core beliefs about what is meaningful and important offer a stable reference point in times of struggle. Aligning our actions to what matters helps us work through confusion and maintain direction with greater resolve during difficult times. A commitment to integrity helps guide us to make an ethical decision under pressure. Dedication to our family can inspire us to persevere for their sake. Values transform turmoil into a journey of self-discovery and strength.

5. Lean on relationships

We are rarely alone when facing challenges. Who are your mentors or allies? What have they said about the situation you are in? Have you taken time to reflect on their advice or are you rushing past the wisdom they are offering? We often make our worst decisions on our own. You don't need to agree with everyone you talk to, but it can be a mistake to hide the situation you are in from the people you trust.

These ideas are not exhaustive, and they will prove most beneficial when you apply them to a specific context. Why not give one or two a try using a problem you are facing right now? The specific ideas are of little importance. What matters is that when you feel stuck you find a perspective that helps you move forward. It may not be obvious, and I'm not saying it will always be easy, but there is always a way forward if you are willing to see it.

The power of perspective

Finding perspective is the most fundamental of all the practices presented in this book. You cannot take control of your life until you decide you are in charge. Recognise that you get to choose the perspective you bring to every situation.

You might not be able to change your circumstances or the obstacles you face, but how you see a situation influences how easy or difficult it is for you to engage with and overcome. Whether you bring confusion or confidence to the picture. Whether you come to the situation from a position of weakness or a position of strength. Whether you choose to define the situation or let it define you.

Your perspective frames your experience.
Please choose yours wisely.
A great life depends on it.

Insight → Action

Premise

Our lives rarely unfold according to plan. You won't see each frustrating event, unexpected challenge or obstacle coming. But you have more control over them than you think and can always turn them into something.

Practice

When you next face a situation that feels frustrating or overwhelming, pause and ask yourself: *What opportunity is hidden in this problem?* Not to be blindingly positive, but to genuinely look for what might be useful. This might be a personal insight, a change to make or a lesson you need to learn. Something that enables you to make the mental shift from seeing the problem to sourcing a solution.

Promise

Problems that get put under pressure ultimately break apart. By consistently seeing possibilities within problems, you give your life maximum leverage by developing the mental flexibility to turn any setback into something better.

3

Unlock

Surface your stories

Fit in. For most of my early life, that's what I tried to do most. Growing up as the son of a church minister, I spent my childhood following Dad to the various postings he was given by the church. A new congregation for Dad meant a new school for me – often in the middle of the year when classes were settled, friendship groups were formed and student inductions had all been done.

As a new kid I learnt an important lesson in those early years. The laws of the playground are like the laws of the jungle. If you want to stay safe, you need to fit in with the herd. Turns out that having people to work with, eat lunch with, play with and walk between classes with shelters you from the attention of bullies who are eager to pick on anyone who was isolated, defenceless or different. I learnt how to be interesting enough for people to accept me into their group but submissive enough to maintain the social hierarchy that had already been established.

A safe place where I was protected by the crowd.

And it worked. My high school days were mostly hassle free. But over time, being a master at fitting in stopped serving me. The pattern of behaviour that once protected me so well started impacting my ability to live a meaningful life. My self-protection story from high school was subconsciously coercing me to fit in and stay safe, with messages such as: 'Just smile and nod, Andrew.' 'I'm not sure people will agree with that idea.' 'You're not as good as Brett.' 'Just feign interest to keep the conversation going. It would be foolish to contradict the most powerful person in the room.'

I was no longer living my life. I was living a curated version that was being held captive by a subconscious story that was no longer relevant or helpful.

The power of stories

We make sense of the world through stories. While some of these stories are within our awareness, others are hidden away, formed in our early years and long since forgotten. Think about some of the early influences that shaped your life experience growing up. What was the family context you grew up in? What messages did your parents reinforce during conversations at the dinner table? Did they value your academic results or the effort you applied? How did your parents manage stress, pressure and failure? What about the work culture you experienced early in your career? How did that shape your beliefs about work and how you should be treated in the workplace?

Contemplating questions like these helps to provide an understanding of how your experiences, positive or otherwise, have shaped your story. The narrative you have created about how to survive, stay connected and get ahead in the world.

We forge our identity through the stories we tell. These stories can be wise, resourceful and affirming; encouraging you to take a confident stride towards the things you desire. But they can also be misguided and overprotective, creating unnecessary fears and anxieties that cause you to jump at shadows and hold you back. Just like my self-protective story from school impeded the progress of my career.

If you have ever wondered why you feel stuck or what stops you from making a positive change to your life, the answer lies somewhere in your stories.

The paradox of protection

We don't often consider our stories when it comes to making change. We tend to set a goal and take actions we believe will help us achieve that goal. Rarely do we take the time to explore our identity or the underlying beliefs and assumptions driving our behaviour that can sometimes sabotage the change we are trying to make. It's a recipe for frustration and failure.

A lesson Liam is in the process of learning.

Liam feels anxious. His mind is blank, and he can feel his heart thumping in his chest. Trying to appear relaxed, he reads over his notes as hundreds of people take their seats to hear what the new Executive Director of Housing has to say. Gripping the lectern like his life depends on it, he looks up at the large crowd and feels nauseas. Liam is a brilliant and personable leader – but he hates public speaking. Right before he begins, his inner critic starts to chatter.

'What are you doing?'

'This isn't what you're good at.'

'Why did you think you could pull this off?'

'You'll make a fool of yourself in front of these people.'

This inner voice distracts him and erodes his confidence. Liam struggles through his sixty-minute presentation, missing the opportunity to make a real impact. Afterwards, in the comfort of his office, nursing a drink and the sting of disappointment, Liam wonders how he will overcome his fear of public speaking. In his new role, with the organisation facing unprecedented challenge and change, speaking in front of a large group will be a weekly occurrence.

Later that evening, after catching up on the day's events with his two children, Liam discusses his concerns with his wife, Lucy.

'I don't know if I can do this new leadership role. Maybe I should go back to a more operational role that better suits my skills. If I freeze during presentations, my career will hit a dead end. I mean, small groups are fine, but what is it about the larger groups that make me feel so apprehensive and nervous?'

Despite his good intentions, without help Liam will stay stuck because he thinks he has a speaking problem when, in fact, he has a story problem. Since his father continually criticised his ideas and efforts when Liam was young, he has a deep need to be seen in a favourable light. Especially in the context of work, where he needs to be seen as capable and competent. The new role, and addressing a larger audience, amplifies the risk to Liam's reputation, igniting his evolutionary bias to prioritise self-protection over self-expression.

That's why his internal critic started speaking up. It was warning him of the potential danger he was facing – bombing the speech and being seen in an unfavourable light. The challenge Liam faces in becoming a better public speaker is not about his ability to present. It's about rewiring the story trying to protect him from the failure and humiliation he experienced as a child.

If you are stuck in a situation you don't want to be in, you need to conduct a certain level of excavation on your life. Reflect on your past experiences and work out how they might be triggering unhelpful patterns that keep you stuck. What are the stories you are walking around that drive your behaviour? Are they helpful? Are they true? Do they empower you?

You can read books, listen to podcasts and attend courses, but if you are not reckoning with your stories you will stay stuck in your current paradigm, unable to recalibrate your life around a better trajectory.

Surface your stories

To make significant change, you need to surface the stories keeping you stuck. Sometimes these stories are subtle. Sometimes they are intense. Sometimes you know they exist. Sometimes they are hidden deep in your subconscious.

Building awareness – reflecting on your life to see what it's trying to tell you – helps surface your stories.

If that seems scary or you experienced some kind of trauma early in your life, I recommend you seek professional counselling rather than trying to reflect and make sense of things on your own. Otherwise, the guided steps on the following pages will help surface your unhelpful stories and recalibrate their meaning to better serve the change you are trying to make.

1. Choose what to change

First, make sure you are clear about a change you *want* to make. Something important that would be significant if it were to improve. What is an unhelpful behaviour you want to address? How about an ongoing issue you haven't resolved? Is there a courageous step you have been delaying but want to take? Whatever you decide, your goal for improvement needs to focus on you and the changes you need to make. Liam chose: *To be a better presenter (by staying calm, staying present, and focusing on my message) so I have greater impact and enjoy my new leadership role.*

2. Identify contradictory actions

Now make a mental list of all the things you are doing (or not doing) that work against the goal you are trying to achieve. The more concrete behaviours you can list, the better. Liam initially said, *I feel uncomfortable speaking in front of larger groups*. This response isn't ideal because it reflects his state of mind rather than his behaviour. Delving deeper to explore what he does or feels because of his discomfort enabled more helpful responses, like, *I focus my attention on the audience, not my speech* and *I rely heavily on my notes and tend to read my presentation*. The more honest you make this list, the greater level of transformation you will experience.

3. Explore underlying fears

To make progress, you must connect with the unconscious fears that work against the change you are trying to make. Generating this raw data can be difficult, so for each thing you listed in the previous step, ask: *What is the outcome I am most worried or feel uncomfortable about?* For example, Liam said: *I'll feel stupid. People won't respect me. I'll lose credibility* and *I'll feel unimportant and worthless*. These fears, while intending to protect him, created enormous anxiety and pressure, robbing Liam of the focus he needed to deliver a successful presentation. The impact of Liam's self-protection story – needing to always be seen in a favourable light – started to emerge. Focus on your own fears and let your subconscious mind start to reveal your own protective story.

4. Surface your protection story

Your self-protection story will be starting to emerge. If you have more than one, identify which is the most powerful and focus on that for now. Surfacing your story means you can rewrite it and are less likely to be captive to it in the future. Exploring the following questions relating to your responses in the previous step may help you identify the threads of your underlying story.

What tenderness or fragility are you protecting?
What story about yourself is no longer serving you?
To feel worthy I must always/never...
Who are you becoming doing what you are doing?
What are you paying attention to? Why does it matter?
What is your hidden or unspoken motivation?

5. Write a more supportive story

You may be eager to rewrite your story after identifying the ways you prevent your own progress and success. But your mind is sharp and will quickly discount any approach based on positive self-talk and motivational hot air. The new story you tell needs to be real and reinforce the change you are trying to make, while acknowledging the protective intent of your original story. Here's how we applied this approach to Liam's story: *Thanks for trying to protect me when I feel pressure to be seen in a favourable light, but I am a strong and capable leader with a great track record. I don't need protecting right now.*

6. Experiment with your new story

It would be naive to think rewriting your story will automatically result in a change of behaviour. Your subconscious mind will need to be convinced that your new story can protect you sufficiently from the anxiety and fear you felt in the first place. To do this, think about how and when your old story surfaces and the feelings that arise when it occurs. This will help prime your brain to the situations when you need to activate your new, more helpful story. Pick situations that won't have catastrophic consequences if it doesn't work out the way you hope, and test your new story in these situations.

7. Measure and evaluate your progress

Liam tested out his new story before every big presentation and prior to making contributions in meetings where he felt his reputation was at risk. Not everything he tried worked. Which is why measuring and evaluating progress is so important. It allows insights to be gained, your story to be refined and progress to be maintained, so you achieve the long-term change you are trying to make. How this is achieved will depend on the type of change you are undertaking. For Liam, we tracked how often he used his new story over a four-week period, using 'sometimes', 'often' and 'most of the time' as a simple rating system.

Working to free yourself from your unhelpful stories – choosing to hold onto your stories a little less tightly so you define yourself *not* by your past but the future you seek to build – is an act of positive rebellion.

Surfacing your stories isn't just about understanding yourself. It's about freeing yourself to navigate the messy middle without the invisible chains of old narratives. When you rewire your stories, you rewire your capacity to handle difficulty.

Find your freedom

It may take years, even decades, to surface your hidden stories, created by a critical parent, a throwaway line delivered in the playground or a mistake you haven't forgiven yourself for. These are experiences you have internalised and need to examine in order to detach from the stories that no longer serve who you want to be.

It's tempting to pretend you have less control than you do. Life is much less confronting that way. But most people have more control over the narrative of their lives than they give themselves credit for, and how much you prosper or struggle is primarily based on the story you tell.

Insight ⤻ Action

Premise

We carry beliefs about who we are and what we're capable of from stories that were formed long ago. We often forget where they came from, and rarely notice them subconsciously running our lives. To make significant change, you need to surface the stories that are keeping you stuck.

Practice

Whether it's during a meeting or family meal, prior to a big presentation or driving in the car, pay attention to the stories you are telling yourself. The conversations you have with yourself, about yourself or the situation you are in. Are the stories true? Or are they overly protective and preventing you from making forward progress?

Promise

Working to free yourself from unhelpful stories is an act of positive rebellion. You become unstuck and navigate the messy middle more effectively, without your overprotective stories getting in the way.

4

Evolve

Pursue continual growth

Oscar McMahon was about to lose everything.

As one of the founders of Young Henrys, a craft brewery in Sydney's inner west, Oscar and his other partners had spent eight years building the business. The brand was synonymous with Sydney's creative culture. Their beers were featured in most local pubs – and the taproom had become a neighbourhood gathering spot for locals.

Then the pandemic hit.

Overnight, bars and restaurants closed. The festivals, where Young Henry had gained much of their following were cancelled. The taproom, usually buzzing with locals, sat eerily empty and within seven days sales had plummeted by 70 per cent. Eight years of hard work evaporating in what felt like eight minutes.

'We were terrified,' Oscar told me when I spoke with him on Episode 32 of *The Messy Middle* podcast. 'Twenty-five families relied on us for their income, and we had no idea if we could keep paying them. Each night I'd stare at the ceiling wondering if this was how it would all end.'

The obvious path was to hunker down, cut costs and hope to weather the storm. Many micro-breweries did just that. Most didn't survive. But as Oscar and his team assessed the situation, they noticed something peculiar happening globally. Distilleries were transitioning production to make hand sanitiser, which had become hard to find as panic buying cleared shelves.

Oscar and his team decided to pivot.

While the Young Henrys equipment wasn't designed for sanitiser, they knew they had the scientific knowledge, food grade facilities and distribution networks that could be repurposed. Within a week, they had partnered with a local gin distillery, converted part of their brewery, and were producing World Health Organization formula sanitiser for frontline workers.

'We'd never considered making anything but beer and gin,' Oscar said. 'But adapting meant we kept our staff employed, served our community when they needed us most and discovered new capabilities we never knew we had.' Young Henrys didn't just survive. They thrived.

Their community connections deepened, the team became more resilient and they found new revenue streams that carried them through the pandemic. When they eventually returned to beer production, Young Henrys wasn't the same company. It was stronger, more adaptable and clearer about its purpose.

Like many of their competitors in the pandemic, Young Henrys could have decided to close. Instead, they chose to evolve.

Easier said than done

Accepting the challenge to evolve and then looking back on what you were able to achieve is fantastic. When you are in the messy middle though? That can be more difficult, because our brain conspires against us when we put ourselves out there for something we care about. You experience this in the flutter in your stomach when suggesting something new, the tightness in your chest before you leap, or your legs feeling like lead right before the start of the race. These are your natural survival instincts sensing danger, telling you to retreat to where things are familiar, predictable and safe.

We can often get stuck when we mistake these warning signs as danger rather than discomfort, and coordinate life around a comfort zone that isn't quite bold enough. This is the kind of mistake that nearly derailed the career of Johnny Cash.

In 1954 Cash walked into the recording studio at Sun Records having secured a spot to play for renowned record producer Sam Phillips. At the time, Cash was a nobody. He was selling appliances door to door and playing gospel songs at night. He was broke, and his marriage was in ruins. Playing for Phillips was his break. But instead of going for broke, Cash decided to sing a gospel song for his audition. It was what he knew best and gospel was all the rage in 1954. Everyone was singing it.

As depicted in the movie *Walk the Line*, the audition didn't go as Cash had planned. As he begins to sing a dreary gospel song, the record label owner, Sam Phillips, feigns interest for 30 seconds before interrupting. He says he's heard this song numerous times before, sung by other gospel singers in the exact same way that Cash sang it. Telling Cash, 'I don't make music that doesn't sell', Phillips gives Cash a lifeline, asking him to sing something different. A song of redemption that comes from his heart. 'It ain't got nothing to do with believing in God, Mr Cash,' Phillips says. 'It has to do with believing in yourself.'

This berating jolts Cash out of his conformist, let-me-sing-you-some-good-old-gospel attitude. It brings out the part of him that's been buried by a crushing mortgage, a stale marriage and too many years in the air force. He collects himself, starts strumming his guitar and begins singing 'Folsom Prison Blues'. In that moment, he stops trying to be a gospel singer, and becomes Johnny Cash.

The real danger is not failing or looking foolish. It's looking back with pain or regret about the things we could have been or done. We assume that following the herd makes us safe, so rather than stand for something we choose to sing gospel, unaware of the impact of staying in our comfort zone under the guise of protection.

The days blend together and years rush by, until one day you look back and see your life is defined not by what you did but by what you didn't do. The risks you didn't take. The conversations you avoided. The dreams you deferred. The deep regret that you didn't become the person you could have been.

The antidote to stagnation

Your dreams often need different skills. The skills that make you a valuable contributor aren't necessarily the same as those that will make you a great leader. The relationship approaches that work in dating don't always translate into building a successful relationship. The habits that keep you healthy in your thirties need to be modified in your fifties.

This is the paradox that stops us moving forward.

We want change but resist changing.

We want the corner office but spend more time fitting in than forging a reputation for valuable work. We want more fulfilling relationships but avoid the vulnerability that's needed to create them. We want financial freedom but maintain spending habits that hinder our capacity to save. We set goals but ignore achieving them requires us to evolve and become someone new. Someone with capabilities, perspectives and experience we may not currently possess. But there is one important catch. You have to do the work.

You can organise as many offsites, listen to as many podcasts and attend as many workshops as you like, but all the ideas in the world are useless if you don't do the work. If you don't commit to the uncomfortable experience of feeling unsure, trying something new or taking a stand to make something happen. Building your better future will prove elusive until you confront the void between where you are and where you want to be. And until you commit to the course of action that requires some guts but has the potential to change everything.

It's common for us to assume that what makes us comfortable also makes us safe. Johnny Cash made that mistake and nearly squandered his big break. If you want to advance personally or professionally, there is a new truth you must be prepared to embrace: it's better to be sorry than safe.

Escaping stuck

There's a scene in *The Shawshank Redemption* when Morgan Freeman's character is finally released from prison after spending most of his life there. One of the saddest scenes in the movie is when he asks the manager of a grocery store where he works if he can go to the bathroom. Irritated by the request, his boss calls him over and tells him he doesn't need to ask every time he needs to go to the bathroom. He says, 'Just go. Understand?'

While I assume you've never been to prison, you probably have friends to whom you want to say, 'Just go!' You can see them making the same mistake again and again. The person they keep complaining about, the bad job they never leave or their lousy attitude that keeps inviting trouble – over time your compassion turns to frustration because they are choosing to stay stuck.

If you're not stuck right now, brilliant. Keep evolving and sharpening your skills to prevent yourself becoming stuck. But if you are stuck in a situation you want to escape, here are three perspectives worth considering to build a better future.

1. Future > Past

We get stuck by using the past as our primary reference point for what we think is possible. Being too connected to past successes, painful failures or patterns of behaviour can often place a ceiling on our potential. Making your future greater than your past helps to shift your mindset from past experiences to future possibilities. Which starts by reflecting on the situations, relationships and activities currently keeping you stuck.

+ What do you long for or want to pursue?
+ What is stopping you from making a start?
+ How could you overcome those constraints?
+ Who can help (or is hindering) your success?
+ How would a forward focus improve your life?

2. Confidence > Comfort

Evolving requires us to stretch beyond where we have been before. Many of us start off as dreamers and risk takers, but the moment we become successful we seek out security and comfort to protect what we have achieved. Over time, we lose the very confidence that created our success in the first place. Making your confidence greater than your comfort means letting go of what's lulling you to sleep motivationally by taking on a new challenge.

+ How is your relationship with failure?
+ What success are you currently protecting?
+ What action would reignite your passion or purpose?
+ How could you reclaim your risk-taking mindset?
+ How would taking more risks improve your life?

3. Learning > Experience

You can have a great deal of experience but not be any smarter for all the things you have done, seen and heard. Every experience we have has two parts: what worked and what didn't. When you turn these experiences into new learning, every day becomes a source for improvement. New, more effective ways of working become possible, enabling experiences to become sources of growth.

+ What learning did you overlook from a recent challenge?

+ How is your approach keeping you stuck in the same situation?
+ How could you implement a daily practice of deliberate learning?
+ Where are you accumulating experience but stagnating in your skillset?
+ How can you source lessons learnt from your everyday experiences?

What waits for you on the other side of these questions? Everything that matters to you. Your unlived life. The career that fulfils you. The relationship that completes you. The opportunities you can't yet even imagine. The other side is where your resilience is forged and your true capabilities start to reveal themselves. Each evolution you choose to make – big or small – rewires your brain and expands what you believe to be possible.

Escaping stuck

We all get stuck sometimes.

While the situations in this chapter may not directly reflect your life circumstances, everyone faces obstacles in everyday life. At some point in your day, your train could be late, your project might hit a major hurdle or an unknown virus might turn into a pandemic, throwing your personal and professional life into chaos.

In times of challenge and change, your happiness often hinges on your ability to change at the speed of life. Be careful if you find yourself failing to evolve. Bitterness grows quickly in the quiet corners of comfort.

But it doesn't have to, of course.

You can choose to evolve.

Choosing any one of the four practices that make up character can help you navigate most of the messy middles you find yourself in. Knowing what matters to you helps. Reframing obstacles as opportunities helps. Understanding the stories that have shaped you helps, and so does committing to growth.

But character alone is not enough. You also need capability, which is what we will look at next.

Insight ⤻ Action

Premise

Life rarely stands still. Your organisation announces a restructure. Your family faces an emergency. Your industry shifts. In the modern world we live in, your happiness often hinges on your ability to change at the speed of life.

Practice

Ask yourself with one change you are trying to make: what capability do I need to develop to succeed? Not to be perfect, but to allow yourself to move forward. Start there. Just one skill. One idea. One new practice. One deliberate action that helps you successfully navigate the situation you are in.

Promise

Your ability to adapt determines how well you navigate challenge and change. Resilience is built by developing new capabilities in response to life's demands. Each evolution you make, big or small, will rewire your brain and expand what you believe to be possible.

Capability

You'll never plough a field by
turning it over in your mind.

IRISH PROVERB

I used to love watching Road Runner cartoons as a kid. After school I would sit on the couch with a glass of milk and a dozen ginger nut biscuits and watch the outlandish ways Wiley Coyote would try to catch his arch nemesis the Road Runner. But he never did.

Wiley was a hopeless predator. He was always looking for the quick win. The easiest way to get what he wanted with the least amount of effort. Instead of creating a plan he can persist with over time, the coyote lurched from one hairbrained scheme to another, usually sourced as a mail order purchase from ACME. His outlandish schemes always ended up in frustration.

Wiley Coyote always survived, but he was often in pain. The pain from hitting a wall at 100 km/hour – or the pain of failing to pull off another of his plans. Despite his consistent effort, it's hard to see Wiley's tactics ever working. He works against the laws of physics, spends money on gimmicks that promise a lot but produce very little, and pursues an outcome where his gain must come at the expense of his adversary. Wiley stays stuck because he fails to see the pattern of his behaviour. His dubious shortcuts, small-minded solutions and repetitive mistakes are failing to make an impact.

We are all a little more Wiley than we'd like to admit.

We sometimes look for shortcuts, take the easy option or choose responses that are incongruent with our aspirations or ambitions. We fight with our partner over pointless disputes for the sake of being right. We choose to work extra hours and miss putting our kids to bed. We get short with someone for a mistake they made. We lack the energy and spark to pursue our dreams and desires.

We use excuses as our defence when we behave like Wiley.

We relocate responsibility for our success and happiness to someone or something else. We blame others and fret about trivial details instead of investing our capability to pursue what matters. Making the disciplined decisions and doing the *actual* work that would deliver the result we desired.

As Jason Fried and David Heinemeier Hansson explain in their book *Rework*, 'Many amateur golfers think they need expensive clubs. But it's the swing that matters, not the club. Give Tiger Woods a set of cheap clubs and he'll still destroy you. We don't want to put in the hours on the driving range, so we spend a ton in the pro shop.' We look for shortcuts.

We don't need to wait until we have equipment, time, resources or approval to start making a meaningful contribution. Making a difference and living a meaningful life is doing the best you can with what you have. The courage to make a start and scale as you go.

Tim, a client of mine, got a new job. He didn't leave the organisation, get a new role or new responsibilities. And he wasn't in danger of losing his job either. He was good at his job and doing well. He did his work, delivered what his clients wanted and got paid what he was worth. But Tim had plateaued. He had lost his energy and enthusiasm for work. Tim came to me for help. Over nine intensive coaching conversations, he realised the once bright lights of his role in life had dimmed.

So I helped Tim see things differently. He started doing his old job in a new way. He began to take control of his calendar. He shared his ideas and welcomed debate. He stopped blaming and started collaborating. Tim carved out time for his most important work. He started to go home on time. He ditched his device on the weekend. He was present at home. He prioritised sleep. He became a better person.

Eight weeks later, he received a large internal promotion. Tim now leads a marquee project for a global tech giant. And it all started with him deciding to stand up, speak up and start to do a better job at his current job. The opportunities arose and his life improved, because he committed his skills to where he could make a difference.

Making a contribution is how you create a meaningful life.

Applying the assets you have acquired over time to get things done. The only way to become an author is to write. The only way to finish a marathon is to run. The only way to connect in conflict is to care. You might dread the writing or the running or the caring, but doing the work provides the most direct path to all success and achievement.

Making a personal impact we are proud of means moving beyond where we have been before. We need to stretch our skills and build capability that enables us to take on new challenges. This is easy to say but often hard to do. We often start off as a mover, shaker and risk-taker. But when we start to experience success, we can be prone to prioritising safety to protect what we have worked hard to achieve.

Our capability can easily start to fall asleep at the wheel.

My assumption, if you are reading this book, is that you want more. You have a desire to contribute. You are ready to learn and grow. You want to shake things up and be a force for change. And you are ready to begin. Ready to be a little less Wiley in the way you go about your work. Which matters, because the world needs your capability.

We need more happy marriages. We need more kids seeing their parents at night. Organisations need more leaders we admire and want to emulate. And you need the energy and vitality to fulfil your dreams. This section isn't about saving the world. It's about making a difference.

Where can you move things forward? Make an impact?

Create something new? Shift the balance? Build stronger connections? Improve your life? You don't have to do all these things. One will do.

The opportunities are all around you.

This section will help you take them.

Turn the page and let's begin.

5

Activate

Make things better

I was waiting for my flight to take off, talking with the man sitting next to me. Mark was a retired professional athlete who had a reputation for being fearless on the field. Having transitioned out of football, he was starting his second career as a mortgage broker. A sponsor from his playing days had offered him the job and he'd taken it.

Mark was charismatic and friendly, but as we talked I could sense his deep frustration. His employer, despite having a superstar on their hands, was failing to capitalise on his personality and strengths. The company provided him with weak leads and insisted he use their generic, bland business cards, marketing materials and rigid sales script. Mark, the well-known athlete, was being forced to operate like an anonymous salesman.

He knew he could do better and believed he had the reputation, contacts, and personality to build a thriving business. But he felt stuck. Being wired to help, I started asking some questions. 'Why not use your own network? Create your own marketing materials that leverage your personal brand? Ditch the script and just be you?' And that's when he floored me.

Mark, the man who attacked the football with commitment and courage, started telling me all the reasons why he couldn't change. Why he couldn't deviate from the company's approach. Couldn't possibly leverage his contacts. Why he couldn't question the system, even though he knew it was failing him. He rationalised that if he just kept his head down and put in the hours, things would eventually work out.

This never ceases to amaze me. Here was a man who was 90 per cent of the way to a wildly successful second career but was paralysed by the last 10 per cent. The part where he had to put himself on the hook for the life he had just spent half an hour telling me he wanted. His employer had hired a lion and was trying to make him a lamb, and Mark was letting them.

Mark was a powerful person choosing to be powerless. It's a choice so many of us sadly make. We play it safe, spending too much time complaining about *how things are* rather than creating *how we want them to be.*

A recipe for frustration, failure and regret.

If your life agenda isn't inspiring you or leading you in the direction you want to go, why are you letting it be your agenda? The longer you deny the life you truly want to live, the longer it will elude you. By changing the status quo, you can be the person you want to be, live the kind of life you are meant to live and make the kind of contribution you know you are capable of.

The choice is yours. Every single day.

Do the work

We often think that to make things better or improve our life in some way, we need more time, more money, more opportunity or more clarity. In reality, what our dreams really need is more action. In the movie *Rocket Man*, there's a scene where a young Elton John plays the piano for a touring band. Backstage after the show, Elton asks the lead singer, 'How do I get to be a songwriter?' To which the lead singer replies, 'Write some songs.'

Go do the work. That's pretty good advice.

The chasm between wanting to and willing to is huge. We often want the job title or life change without the work. We want to be an entrepreneur, but don't build anything. We want to be a podcaster, but don't record anything. We want to get promoted, but don't stand for anything.

To do something meaningful and make life count, the barrier to success is rarely a lack of opportunity, the difficulty of the task, the state of the market or the bottom line on our bank account. The barrier is usually fear. We are scared of being wrong, being judged or lacking experience. Listening too much to our fear makes us doubt and delay, which keeps us stuck.

Choosing to pursue what we care about promotes progress and helps us get unstuck. Moving forward in our lives is rarely achieved by buying a book, taking a course, purchasing a product or researching the right approach to take. You progress when you take the step that moves you closer to the way you want things to be. And inevitably this means doing things differently.

Maybe you'll need to be more assertive than feels comfortable. Maybe you'll have to be less collaborative than you usually are. Perhaps you need to ignore the rules or ask for forgiveness rather than permission. To achieve what you are capable of, you must move beyond what you are comfortable doing. Stepping into your discomfort to overcome an obstacle or expand your horizons builds the assets that bring your aspirations to life.

This is the messy middle: the gap between knowing what needs to be done and actually doing it. Sometimes, this presents as a positive opportunity. Most of the time however, the results we seek are disguised in difficult and demanding work. Work we choose to seek out if success is a serious aspiration, because we understand that the struggle isn't a problem to overcome. It's a practice to engage in, in order to become someone capable of living the life they want.

Lessons from The Wiggles

In the late 1990s, The Wiggles knew they had a winning formula. The four Australian friends in brightly coloured skivvies had turned a university project into a national treasure, selling out concert halls and dominating children's television. They knew their unique, education-based approach to entertainment worked and, like many talented artists who are good at what they do, wanted to be better. So they decided to conquer America.

There was just one small problem.

Their success in Australia meant nothing.

At the first gig they played, The Wiggles discovered that their accents were more of a barrier than they had imagined they would be, and the structure and style of their performance was a mystery to American audiences. They knew they had a great product but they failed to connect.

This is the kind of moment that tests us all. When you know you have something to offer, but you can't seem to make it work. The moment when we realise there is a gap and have to be willing to accept our reality to overcome the gap.

Which is exactly what The Wiggles did.

They identified the gaps in their approach and took specific, deliberate actions to close them. They knew they needed a partner who understood the American market, so they swallowed their pride and teamed up with the producers of *Barney & Friends* to perform as the opening act. They knew they needed to build an audience from scratch, so they played in church halls and tiny 500-seat theatres, grinding it out, one small audience at a time. They knew they needed to adapt their show for a new culture, so they studied how American children responded and tweaked their performances, making them more interactive and dynamic.

They didn't abandon who they were or what they stood for. They kept their skivvies, their accents and their commitment to the early childhood principles that underpinned their shows. But they *were* willing to change how they performed. They were willing to be humble, willing to learn and willing to do the unglamorous work of addressing the gap between their ambition and their reality. Their hard work eventually paid off in the most unusual circumstances.

Weeks after the September 11 attacks in 2001, a wave of fear and uncertainty swept through America. Concerts were cancelled as performers chose to stay at home. But The Wiggles, who were scheduled to perform in New York, made a different choice. They played their shows. They brought a small measure of joy and normalcy to a city shrouded in grief. By showing up when others wouldn't, they made their final important transition: from being a visiting act to a trusted friend.

That was their turning point. Shortly after, they were selling out Madison Square Garden and their videos were all over the Disney channel. The Wiggles music had become the soundtrack of the lives of millions of American kids. They had finally conquered America. Not with one giant leap but with a series of small, deliberate and courageous steps. Steps that reinforced who they were while acknowledging the parts that were preventing them from achieving the ambition they had set out to achieve.

Something Mark seemingly still had to learn.

And perhaps something you need to remember too.

The Wiggles didn't avoid the messy middle. They walked directly into it. They identified gaps, humbled themselves, did unglamorous work, adapted and persisted. They're not a success story despite the difficulty. They're a success story *because of* the difficulty. The struggle to close the gap between their ambition and reality is what built the capability they needed.

When you feel stuck, you can let your gaps gets wider, or you can push yourself to close them so you can be the person you know you can be.

Uncomfortable truths

Right now there is a gap between where you are and where you want to be. Maybe you are financially stretched and feel under pressure or wish you could take a holiday without the work piling up while you're away. Perhaps your backhand volley needs work or you can't get your kids to use their cutlery.

This gap is a natural part of your progression and growth. It exists because you desire something to be better.

And it's one of the conversations I love most as a coach. Helping people close the gap between their intention and action. Establishing a suitable level of rapport and trust that enables clients to interrogate the *internal* obstacles holding them back and keeping them stuck.

External obstacles are easy to identify. We rarely have a problem blaming our colleagues, the market, our lack of time or adequate resources for making life hard. It's much harder allocating our lack of progress or success to a short fuse, poor lifestyle, lack of patience or low self-esteem.

I work with clients to identify these internal obstacles, the uncomfortable truths about the situation where they feel stuck. Uncomfortable, because they start to see the reality of what they find difficult and why. And truths, meaning they don't deny the specific behaviours occur.

Uncovering your uncomfortable truths is a powerful process to identify the internal obstacles you may have missed or not yet addressed that are causing you to feel stuck in your personal or professional life.

I ask my clients to answer the following sentence as openly and honestly as possible:

> I'd like to ________________, but if I am being honest, it's an uncomfortable truth that ______________________.

The uncomfortable truth for an AFL player might be they have a poor performance record in big games. A salesperson's uncomfortable truth might be that they rarely make their quarterly target. A parent's uncomfortable truth might be that they routinely yell at their kids whenever they are tired or stressed.

The purpose of this process isn't to highlight a personality flaw or inability to perform. It's about drawing attention to the intrinsic obstacles keeping you from doing the work you know needs to be done and ultimately escape the situation you're stuck in. Looking at reasons for a lack of action in this way humanises struggle and helps navigate difficult circumstances by respectfully drawing attention to the areas you might typically avoid.

If you are serious about pursuing better and reaching your potential, you need to become aware of the actions you are avoiding. Identifying your uncomfortable truths is not always easy or enjoyable, but it's liberating. Once you see what's holding you back, you can do something about it. And when you do something about it, you close the gap between where you are and where you want to be and build the life you want.

Not a life that looks better.

A life that *is* better.

Quieten the critic

Now, if you're feeling motivated to take control of your life and start your business, curb your spending or be a better parent, be prepared. Your inner critic is about to saunter out of the shadows and into your life.

The voice that says you are not entitled to your success. That you've fooled everyone into believing you are more capable than you really are and it's only a matter of time before you get exposed. We all spend more time than we'd like to admit listening to that voice. Listening to the reasons why we should sit down and be quiet, instead of stepping into what we know we should do.

Our inner critic will say anything to undermine our potential. Like a bully in the playground, it will target our deepest insecurities and fears. The areas of our personal and professional life where we most feel undervalued, unappreciated and uncertain.

You know when your critic is lurking in the background. You can hear the negative voice nagging away trying to distract you from doing your work. It's okay to pay attention to that voice. Just don't let it define you.

Taking action quietens our critic because we create a body of work that can easily disprove the claims they are making. When Michael Phelps launched off the blocks at the Olympic 200-metre butterfly final in 2008, his goggles started filling with water. By the 25-metre mark he had zero visibility. Incredibly, Phelps was unperturbed and kept racing. But that wasn't the amazing part.

Hearing his critic chastising his poor preparation, Phelps found composure by stating a fact he could easily recall from his hours of training. He knew exactly how many strokes he took in the first, second, third and fourth 50 of all his best 200 butterfly times. He quietened his critic by reverting to his routine – and it enabled him to focus, break a world record and win a gold medal. That's a level of mental toughness many of us can't even comprehend, let alone emulate. But look more closely and you can see the critical skills we can all practise to quieten our inner critic.

First, he didn't allow a setback that could have easily provoked rage make him angry. He controlled his emotions.

Second, he could have focused his attention on bad luck and cast himself as a victim. He didn't. And finally, he could have easily used the incident as an excuse to resign himself to a poor result. He didn't do that either.

He did the thing our critic hates most.

He took control and put his skills to work.

Make things better

There are countless people who will talk about problems in their daily interactions. You might even be one of them. People who are experts at explaining why something isn't working, what went wrong or why things can't be done. There are fewer people who ask, 'How can we get this done?' or, even better, say, 'Let me take care of that.' People who see a problem and are willing to make a positive contribution.

Be that person.

The one who makes things better.

Vic Firth came up with the idea of making a better drumstick when he was performing with the Boston Symphony Orchestra. The sticks he was using weren't up to the task of performing the more difficult pieces of music he was needing to play. Vic decided to start make his own sticks in his basement at home. He pioneered methods of stick manufacturing including centreless grinding and matching sticks based on moisture content and pitch so they were identical pairs. The result became his product tagline: the perfect pair. Today, Vic Firth are the number one drumstick manufacturer in the world, churning out 12 million sticks each year. Vic's story isn't an isolated one.

James Dyson invented his own vacuum when the bag version he was using at home kept losing suction and wouldn't collect debris and dust. Track coach Bill Bowerman broke his wife's waffle iron trying to create a more lightweight and grippy running sole for Nike. Sarah Blakeley invented Spanx when the pantyhose she wore selling faxes in the hot Florida sun were too uncomfortable.

James, Bill and Sarah aren't superhuman or have something extraordinary that you don't. They are normal people who decided to make things better.

Improving your current circumstances is one of the fastest ways to elevate your life. The meeting you loathe to attend? Make it more beneficial. The infuriating commute you endure every morning? Make it more enjoyable. The relentless pace that tires you every week? Make it more manageable. The chaotic early mornings you confront every day? Make them more orderly.

Making things better means accepting how things are, then taking action to move them closer to how you would prefer them to be. Whether you are leading a team, working to leave a legacy or just trying to get the kids to school on time, committing to the ideas in this chapter will help you succeed.

Ignore them at your peril.

Insight ⤻ Action

Premise

You're waiting for the right conditions, the right resources or the right time to start taking action. Meanwhile, the gap between where you are and where you want to be, or who you are and who you want to be, keeps widening.

Practice

What's one thing you could improve with the time, resources and authority you already have? Don't start with your biggest problem. Start with something small. Make that better. Then notice how good that feels and use the momentum to improve something else. If you do this, you'll build the confidence to tackle bigger changes. You don't need a perfect plan. You just need to start.

Promise

You will feel powerful. Small improvements compound into a sense your life is moving in the right direction. Do that and you quickly become someone who makes things better. Not someone waiting for better things to happen.

6

Optimise

Structure your success

In the 1980s Van Halen was one of the loudest and most forward-thinking rock bands, pushing the boundaries in their live shows. At the time, most rock bands travelled with three trucks of gear. Van Halen used eighteen semi-trailers to carry their colossal stage production, which included 850 lights, miles of cables, hundreds of pyrotechnics and concert staging that rivalled the infrastructure of a small town.

The band's mega-production created real challenges, because the venues they were playing were built decades before anyone dreamed of a concert being delivered at this scale. The arenas simply weren't equipped to handle their gigantic production, with narrow doorways, outdated electrical set-ups and floors that would groan under the sheer weight of the equipment.

David Lee Roth, the band's frontman, knew failing to pay attention to their complex set-up could mean more than a delay – it could mean disaster. The situation was made even more critical by the cowboy promoters, who back then tended to gloss over the crucial set-up requirements included in the contract. To mitigate the issue, buried in the usual specifications in the contract detailing voltage requirements and load bearing capacities, there was a small, seemingly absurd, clause: no brown M&Ms backstage.

If Roth ever walked into a dressing room and saw brown M&Ms, he knew the promoter was unlikely to have read the contract carefully. If they missed the M&Ms, what else might they have overlooked? The electrical set-up? The security of the venue? The structural stability of the stage? If one small detail was ignored, chances were the whole production was compromised. And given the band wanted to deliver a consistently unforgettable experience to their fans, technical mistakes and failures were not an option.

David Lee Roth didn't care about chocolate.

He cared about putting on a kickass rock show.

The brown M&Ms clause wasn't rock-star arrogance, it was a clever early warning detection system designed to make sure the massive show Van Halen performed was never compromised.

Effort isn't effortless

Making the things we want to get done easier makes sense, but we often fail to do that because we are culturally conditioned to work hard for our success. We tend to invest more time and effort to overcome obstacles rather than simply remove them altogether. This approach invites trouble, because we don't have an endless supply of energy throughout the day.

Just like the battery on your mobile phone, you start the day with a certain level of charge and as you go about your day you use up your energy, reducing your level of charge. The more energy you use, the more it gets depleted and the less you have at your disposal. Your energy, just like your mobile phone, has a limited battery life. It's a limited but renewable resource.

Most of us know limited resources need to be managed. But like most busy professionals managing multiple demands throughout your day you probably fail to see your energy as one of these. You rush through the day as though you have endless amounts of energy, rather than seeing it as a resource that needs to be managed, causing you to feel overworked, overwhelmed and tired.

Everything you want in life takes energy.

Getting fit means having the energy to exercise. Being a fantastic parent means having the energy to play. Leading well means having the energy to make wise decisions. Loving well means having energy for your partner. The more difficult you find the task, the more friction you experience – and the more energy you require. When your energy is depleted, you revert to your default settings. Which begs the question: what are your default settings? When your energy is drained, do you reach for a piece of fruit or a bag of chips? Do you stay calm under pressure or lose your cool? Will you concentrate on the work at hand or the distraction that drops in?

David Lee Roth's default response to lacklustre concert preparations was not polite or productive, so he found a better way. As he shared in an interview with MTV, 'Adding the brown M&Ms to our backstage rider allowed us to anticipate roadblocks and protect the quality of our performance. Instead of getting irritable and running around checking every little detail, we could relax and just focus on the parts of the performance that were vital to putting on a good show.'

Most people feel burned out and bring low energy to their most important challenges without realising why life seems so hard. They don't see energy as a resource that gets used up, so end up taking the hardest possible path to success. If you fail to implement strategies that protect your energy, it quickly disappears, making life wildly inconsistent.

Some days you feel like doing the work.

Some days you feel like giving in.

Making the work you want to do easier conserves your energy. The less energy you expend, the more you have at your disposal. And the more likely you are to seize the opportunities in front of you and overcome the challenges life inevitably throws your way.

Reduce the friction

Imagine you are preparing dinner with a blunt knife. You're able to cut, chop and slice, but it requires more effort and the results aren't precise, adding unnecessary tension to the task. Alternatively, by sharpening the knife, you can cut through things effortlessly and cleanly, making the process easier to complete. Rather than working with the friction, you choose to reduce it.

This concept proved useful for entrepreneur Doug Kempel, who was asked to solve a unique problem at Schiphol Airport in Amsterdam. Men were not paying attention when they were going to the toilet, which effected their aim, creating a lot of mess for cleaners. To solve the problem, Kempel simply etched the image of a black housefly onto every urinal within the airport.

According to Kempel, the idea worked because 'it naturally improves a man's aim. When a man notices the fly, he sees it as target, which focuses his attention and increases his accuracy.' He was right. Implementation of the fly in the urinal trial, found the etchings reduced spillage by 80 per cent.

While my urinal etiquette has long been exemplary, I regularly use friction reduction strategies in other areas of my life:

- I break my 2-kilometre swim sessions into 4 x 500 metre splits to make the session feel less mundane.
- When my kids brush their teeth before going to bed, I do too, to help reduce after-dinner cravings.

- My guitar is permanently set up in our parent retreat at home, making it easier for me to pick up and practise more frequently.
- I set an alarm whenever I put anything in the freezer to chill briefly to prevent me forgetting it's there.
- My workday is structured into five two-hour blocks to manage my energy and maximise my productivity.

These are personal examples, but they illustrate the point. We often don't take the time to reflect on the relationship between the effort we are investing and the results we are achieving. But when we do, it doesn't take long to realise that making the work we want to do easier to do is a better blueprint for success than motivation, hard work and hustle.

Being motivated and hard-working are wonderful attributes to have, but they are short-term strategies for success. To achieve in your personal and professional life, you must eliminate as much friction as possible in your day.

Structure your success

I have spent over eighteen years working with highly successful people. While each of their circumstances are different, they all share one similar ingredient when it comes to achieving excellence as well as endurance.

They structure their life to make success easier to achieve.

For Rebecca, structuring her success meant placing her

alarm on the opposite side of the room, because at 6 am she was warm and cozy in bed, and would habitually roll over and press snooze rather than get up and exercise. For Bruce, it meant dedicating the morning to his most important work, so he could maximise his productivity and performance. For Julie, it meant buying a powerbank so her laptop never ran out of charge when she was travelling. Sometimes structuring your success is simply injecting some humour.

That's what Martha Cobbs did. Tired of passengers on Southwest Airlines ignoring her familiar safety announcement monologue, Martha decided to add a few ad-lib lines of her own. When Martha told passengers, 'Put the oxygen mask on yourself first, then place it on your child. If you're travelling with more than one child, start with the one with the greatest earning potential', people laughed. That may not seem like much, but passengers started paying attention, and as Martha continued she had the cabin in hysterics. Passengers started posting recordings of her announcements and Martha quickly became a YouTube sensation. Management loved it so much they encouraged staff to embrace the same humour across their entire fleet. Today economists estimate Southwest Airlines safety announcements have grown revenue by $140 million a year through increased customer loyalty.

Martha made things better by making things funnier. Most people don't do that. When confronting an obstacle or restraint, most people choose to work harder, yell louder or push through, trying to make things better in conditions that make the task harder or more complicated. We try to discipline our kids by yelling at them. We try to lose weight while keeping unhealthy snacks in the pantry. We try to get work done in a chaotic office. We try to be present in close proximity to a smartphone filled with distractions.

It doesn't have to be this way.

We can structure our environment to support our success. The next time you are struggling to get something done, I recommend you stop and ask yourself the following questions:

1. How could this be easier?
2. How could this be simpler?
3. How could this be enjoyable?

If you are a regular business traveller, do you have a physical or digital list of the regular items you need to pack? When you sit down to work, is your workspace clean or full of clutter? If you meet new people regularly, do you have a process to remember and recall their names? What about when you have a really good day – do you journal or record a voicemail message to capture what created your optimism and confidence?

Structuring your success means consciously creating the circumstances to make what you want to do as easy as possible. That's what Martha Cobbs did. She turned a mundane announcement into something worth listening to and skyrocketed the profits of the company. The same is true for you.

If you want to improve your life in some way, your probability for success improves when you make the work easier, simpler or more enjoyable.

Taking the stairs

Imagine you are walking through the train station as you return home on your daily commute. You are tired, checking emails on your phone, when you come across a set of stairs that have been transformed into piano keys.

Every step you take plays a note.

Every step offers a chance to play.

This was the scene commuters encountered at a station in Stockholm, as part of a Volkswagen advertising campaign dubbed Fun Theory. In the video, the company posed the question: can we change behaviour by making it fun?

To exit a train station in Stockholm, commuters could choose to take the stairs or the escalator. Prior to the piano stairs installation, most people chose to take the escalator despite the stairs being a healthier choice. But overnight the Volkswagen team got to work transforming each stair into an individual piano note, like in the 1988 Tom Hanks movie *Big*. Turning the stairs into a musical instrument made something remarkable happen: people stopped opting for the escalator and started to take the stairs.

The once-ignored stairs become the centre of attention. Kids ran up and down trying to play a song with their feet.

Adults broke from routine, smiling and laughing as they stepped with purpose, trying the musical magic beneath their feet. Although walking up the stairs took more effort than standing on an escalator, commuters decided the enjoyment they would gain offset the effort it would take. Making the stairs fun meant 66 per cent more people used them.

But this isn't about stairs and subway stations. It's a powerful example for implementing change. Life is less enjoyable when things are rushed, hard or complicated. If you want to work, lead and live better, make things easier, simpler and more fun.

Insight ⤻ Action

Premise

If you reduce the friction in your daily activities, you burn less brainpower and energy, leaving more mental energy for the times you need it most.

Practice

Look at one thing you consistently do in your day that takes more time or effort than it should. What's making it harder than it needs to be? Remove one piece of friction. Not everything. Just one. Making the work you want to do, easier to do, means you rely less on willpower, so are more likely to get it done.

Promise

With more energy at your disposal throughout the day, you are more likely to seize the opportunities in front of you, and overcome the challenges life will inevitably throw your way.

7

Energy

Sustain your energy

Peter looks like he has barely slept in months. His eyes are red, the skin is sagging around his jowls, and the usual spark he has in his eye, has dimmed. The vibrance and energetic outlook he often possesses is noticeably absent. During our coaching session he leans forward and says to me, 'Andrew, if I keep this pace up, I'm going to break down or have a heart attack.'

'That's not a great outcome, Peter.' I reply. 'No, I know. I need more rest.'

'Yet here we are. You feel tired, look tired and still continue to push.'

'I know. I just need to finish this deal. If I don't, the weeks of work will have been for nothing. When the deal is done, I'll find some time to get away.'

I've heard this promise before. Clients declaring they will rest and take better care of themselves as soon as they land the deal, finish the project or achieve some other illusory performance metric they have set themselves.

But they rarely do. They're always too busy.

Downtime is deeply undervalued today, but it hasn't always been that way. Practically every ancient society defined a good life as balancing work and rest, believing rest strengthened the brain, enhanced learning and stimulated creativity. Many of history's most accomplished scientists, writers, philosophers and military leaders worked fewer hours than we do today. They had daily rituals that were full of downtime. People like naturalist Charles Darwin and artist Pablo Picasso took daily walks, knowing work and rest are not opposites but equal partners. Both are essential for living a happy, healthy life. A concept my client Peter still needed to learn.

Maybe a concept you are struggling with too.

Navigating the messy middle isn't just mentally challenging, it's energetically draining too. You're pushing beyond your comfort zone. You're doing difficult work. You're navigating uncertainty. If you don't actively protect and renew your energy, you'll burn out before you reach the other side. Renewal isn't a luxury. It's a self-care strategy that enables you to sustain your effort during difficult and demanding work.

Feeling exhausted or bordering on burnout?

You need to hustle less and embrace rest.

Audit your energy

Burnout is caused by the emotional exhaustion that comes from being busy without experiencing a sense of meaning or progress. Your emotional resources get depleted coping with challenging situations, competing priorities, putting out spot fires, attending endless commitments and constantly pushing yourself – to the detriment of your health and well-being. Often deferring happiness to a distant horizon you rarely reach.

Reclaiming your vitality starts with rejecting the misconception that work is the sole measure of your value and worth. That overworking should be admired and burnout is the price you must pay for success. I suspect you don't need the latest statistics from Deloitte to know you are working too hard. You can already tell from how little sleep you are getting, how much leave you have accrued and how often you say 'busy' when people enquire about how you are.

We cannot live well if we don't rest well.

Here are five signs you might not usually associate with burnout that indicate your quality of life may be approaching its expiration date:

1. Fading passion

Remember when you played piano, flirted with your partner, noticed the colour of the trees or sang out loud in the car? Passion infuses enthusiasm into the work you are doing, whether that work is managing your career, running your local Auskick or helping your cousin move house. Deep down you know what you are doing matters; you just don't feel it as much anymore. We all experience a loss of passion from time to time, but burnout diminishes your sassiness and spark. It's difficult for a passionless person to live a passionate life.

2. Emotional escalation

Are the little things in life making you disproportionally mad? Someone left their unwashed coffee cup in the communal kitchen. The garage door got stuck and wouldn't open. You misplaced your keys. Problems that would normally be a two or three out of ten have now become an eleven. Turning small things into big things, and thinking big things are small things, is never good. Both are a warning sign something deeper may be wrong.

3. Declining productivity

When you are bordering on burnout your head takes a holiday. Instead of working at your usual pace, everything seems slower and takes longer. Something you may try to fix with even more hustle and hard work. Don't. That will sabotage your life. Use this experience to clarify the contribution you want to make. Declining productivity is also a petri dish for poor decisions. You lose the ability to think clearly. You find yourself taking your frustration out on other people, threatening to quit your job or leaving a nasty note on your neighbour's car.

4. Constantly tired

If you're feeling tired, a good night's sleep or relaxing on the weekend will restore your energy and help you bounce back. If you're burning out, sleep and time off no longer do the trick. In fact, nothing seems to work. Not friends. Food. Exercise. Prayer. Or positive acclamations. This is a time to be careful because this may not just be a busy phase. It may be a sign you are burning out or depressed.

5. Self-medication

Self-medication is the unspoken sign you are struggling. This might involve binge watching, overeating, overworking, drinking too much, impulsive spending or drug use. Hurt and frustration rarely improve when you choose self-medication over self-care. When nothing you do seems to help, the problem isn't external, it's internal. Be honest with yourself and take steps to get the help you need.

You already know these symptoms are counterproductive to living a happy and healthy life. The challenge is awareness. Realising when you have prioritised doing well over being well. One way to make a start is to be mindful of how you are feeling. Next time you wake up tired, skip breakfast, struggle to focus or find yourself snapping at the kids for a silly mistake, take the opportunity to audit your energy. It's hard for burnout to reside in an attentive mind.

The power of rest

I'm not suggesting you don't work hard. The satisfaction you get from pursuing an idea, launching a product, pushing your physical limits or solving a difficult problem is gratifying. I suspect some of the hardest jobs you have ever done have been the most satisfying, because you've had to push boundaries, galvanise a team, challenge the status quo or try something new. Hard work is both honourable and rewarding.

There is merit, however, in taking time to reflect on the relationship between work and rest, to better understand the role they both play in living a productive life. Don't take rest grudgingly, embrace it as an opportunity. When you choose to regularly invest in restorative activities during the day, you are not decreasing your productivity and performance. You are enhancing it.

In an interview on Joe Rogan's podcast, Quentin Tarantino, who has written and directed films like *Pulp Fiction*, *Inglourious Basterds* and *Kill Bill*, was asked to describe his writing process. His response reinforces the power of rest: 'While writing *Inglourious Bastards* I made a change and started writing more during the day. I'd begin around 10:30 am or 11:00 am and write until four, five or six, then stop. Even if I hadn't finished that scene. I'd then hop in my pool and float around in the warm water and think about what I'd just written: going back over it in my head as I floated around in the pool. A lot of things would come to me. So I'd get out of the pool and make little notes, which became my work for the next day. It ended up becoming a really enjoyable, lovely way to write. I was a professional writer before. I just started having a better workday.'

While his earlier career involved long days and pulling all-nighters to finish a script, over time his process matured. He discovered integrating renewal into his work day served his scripts, and his success. Contrary to our corporate and cultural norms, hard work and rest are not opposing forces. They are collaborative partners that help you perform at your peak and reach our goals.

Renewal is not something to do on your weekend or with the leftover hours at the end of your day. Applying restorative strategies throughout the day makes you healthier and happier and helps your mind work better. Taking breaks has been proven to restore your energy, enhance productivity and help you manage the demands of a busy life.

The benefits of renewal only become possible when you stop wearing your work ethic and busyness like expensive jewellery. When you start to pay attention to how your daily rhythms and routines influence your ability to live well, experimenting with your schedule to discover when you are most energised and focused, then tweaking your approach so the rhythms and routines you follow support the person you want to become.

Beating burnout

Sadly, a lot of people only discover the value of rest after a midlife crisis of some kind. If that's you, I'm glad you are reading this chapter now. It's never too late to start making change. And if you are not in crisis but are experiencing some of the warning signs outlined earlier in the chapter, the strategies you are about to read are a better alternative to the inevitable crash you may be approaching.

Beating burnout begins with rest.

Decades of scientific research shows that integrating rest into your day combats fatigue, boosts your mood and lengthens your life. Whether you are an elite coach, corporate CEO, public official or new parent, there are five principles that will help you practise rest more deliberately, improve the quality of your recovery and help you live a more meaningful life.

Energise. Rushing seems like the only option when we are under pressure, but our busiest periods need restorative rest: downtime where you are unreachable and unavailable to clients and colleagues, and even your children. Time where you take a walk outside, eat your lunch in the park, take a break or sit for fifteen minutes with the sun on your shoulders. Activities you find energising and enriching. Self-care is not self-indulgent. It's often the most beneficial rest you can take to restore your energy during times of intense pressure, problems or demand. Something hard-working people with high ambitions can often forget.

Detach. To experience the kind of rest that recharges your body and mind, you need to detach from work. That's difficult to do when you carry the office around in your pocket: when work goes to dinner with you or distracts you while you play with the kids. Not being able to detach defeats the purpose of downtime. Productive rest means putting your phone away and talking about your day over dinner, spending quality time with friends or *actually* taking time off to relax on your holiday. Disconnecting from your device and integrating restorative activities into your day will help you keep work in its rightful place.

Enjoy. People who live long meaningful lives make time for hobbies or interests that give them pleasure. Interestingly, social scientists have found the best hobbies tend to offer the same psychological rewards you get from work, but in a different setting and without the frustrations you face at work. Executives who ride a motorbike, for example, say it combines the focus and problem-solving ability they need to lead with the freedom they want at work. The similarity of skills creates a valuable outlet that helps prevent overworking. Maybe it's time to start those singing lessons?

Escape. Take an honest look at the pace at which you are living right now. Could you do that forever? Would you want to? Feeling tired is not a sign of success. And if you continually say 'it's just a busy period', perhaps it's not a point in time but an unhelpful practice you need to escape. You need a holiday. Ten days is good. A week every three months is better. This doesn't mean spending a week working in a place that just has more sun and sand. Regular holidays where you switch off enable you to return to work resilient, ready to pursue your next opportunity or tackle that tricky obstacle.

Sleep. Sleep plays a vital role in our health and well-being. Observe any high-performance athlete and you will find sleep playing an essential role in their performance. Apart from aiding physical recovery, sleep improves cognitive functions like memory and skill acquisition. Poor sleep, on the other hand, increases the likelihood of stress, anxiety, irritability and poor decision-making. Our brains suffer fatigue just like our bodies do. Instead of investing in more effort and work to be more productive or get things done, embrace the overlooked life hack that has been around as long as you have: a good night's sleep.

It takes hard work to achieve personal and professional success, however you define it. Once you start building some momentum, it can be hard to fight the natural urge to work more and do more, as you try to be more. This is a hazard people with high ambition overlook way too often. Rest is essential for the results you are trying to achieve. That's why learning to do it well is so effective.

Rest and recovery are not mindless activities. They're not happy hour on a Friday night, checking your Facebook feed or catching up with people you can barely tolerate. They're engaging in purposeful activities that are enjoyable, rewarding, sometimes even challenging, that make you happier and healthier and your mind work better.

Sex, singing and running

We live in a world where busyness is worn as a badge of honour. If eight hours of work a day is good, then ten is better and twelve makes us *really* important. Our leisure time is much the same. We pay attention to other people, often following their perfectly filtered Instagram feeds, and feel obliged to keep up. We pack our lives with constant activity to reinforce the perception we are living well.

It doesn't have to be this way.

Running yourself ragged to make yourself feel valued, respected or important will leave you with no time for yourself. While there are people who believe working hard and sleep deprivation are signs of success, others are rejecting this notion. Some people are choosing a different approach that recognises that work and rest are complementary. Both are necessary if you want to live a more creative, productive and meaningful life. Rest is like sex, singing or running. You might have an idea of how to do it, but with a little more understanding and practice you can learn to do it better. You can enjoy your downtime, get better rest and feel more renewed.

There's just one small catch.

Rest is not something you are given. It is something you take.

Don't wait until you have finished all the tasks on your to-do list. Working more doesn't mean you achieve more. Resist the lure to be busy. Build a practice of regular renewal, take it seriously and protect it from a world that is determined to steal it from you.

Insight → Action

Premise

You cannot live well if you don't rest well. Applying restorative strategies throughout the day will make you healthier, happier, and your mind better. Attributes that help manage the demands that come with a busy life.

Practice

It's hard for burnout to reside in an attentive mind. Look at your week. Pay attention to how you are feeling. Where are you spending energy? How are you renewing it? Have you got the balance right? Now protect your renewal like you would a deadline. Schedule it. Guard it. Don't apologise for it.

Promise

You hustle less when you embrace rest. By realising protecting your energy isn't selfish, it's strategic, you will have ample energy to show up fully for the people and places that matter.

8

Support

Recruit some allies

A good ally is someone who will stand beside you and provide counsel, inspiration and advice to help you get things done. Although every ally you have will probably be a friend, not every friend will be a valuable ally. Friends can be fun and enrich our lives, but they aren't necessarily the people you want offering career advice or helping you tackle a prickly problem.

My brother learnt this the hard way.

During a period of his life when he was flipping houses to make some extra income, he asked Dad and I to come over and help him fell a tree. We both agreed, thinking we would be cutting a small sapling with a chainsaw. We were mistaken. The tree was large, standing proudly between my brother's newly renovated kitchen and his neighbour's back garage. It was great fun helping my brother that day, but he never should have asked Dad and me to help fell a tree. He should have asked someone with more skill and expertise. His neighbour, whose garage we partially levelled that day, would agree.

A person with more skills and experience would have said to my brother that trying to pull a 300-kilogram tree away from the house next door with some small ropes and good intentions was asking for trouble. We sure found it that day. You will too if you don't recruit allies who can offer you appropriate help, guidance, and advice.

Working to improve your life in some way can feel isolating. It often means you are working outside your comfort zone, doing things you have never done before, feeling uncertain if you are going to succeed. This is when most people quit. Not because they lack the capability, but because they are trying to navigate change on their own.

Allies change everything.

They provide perspective when you're too close to the problem. They offer encouragement when doubt creeps in. And they remind you why you started when the difficulties you face feel overwhelming.

Success needs support

Over the course of my career, I have coached a lot of people who feel stuck and think their most viable option is to move to another company, relationship, or country. New starts offer new hope, but they are rarely the best option. Sometimes I am the last line of defence before a client decides to do something drastic, like resign or get a divorce. In this situation, at some point during the conversation, I will ask, 'What have the people who advise you said about all this?'

More often than not, there aren't any people. They have no support network helping them navigate their decision. There are cheerleaders who offer support and encouragement with no real discernment. And critics who disparage any attempt they make at progress or change. But there aren't any allies offering valuable advice. My client is stuck, staring into a sea of options, making a huge decision on their own.

As many times as I've advised people who are about to turn their life upside down, I've also sat beside the professional procrastinator. The person who has an exciting opportunity in front of them but are hesitating because they are paralysed by perfectionism and fear. Waiting for all the relevant information or iron-clad guarantee of success, before they commit to a particular course of action. Two different people facing the same dilemma. They both lack allies to go to for advice.

We are not meant to go it alone.

Succeeding or struggling, we need a support network.

Whenever you achieve a level of success and want to continue to prosper, you will find yourself in new situations facing new problems, which typically require new thinking, perspectives and an upgrade of your skills. Escaping your comfort zone to learn new skills is substantially easier, and more enjoyable, if you have support. And, if you are struggling, trying to manage on your own with grit, hard work and hustle, you can feel dejected, disheartened and isolated. Not alone necessarily, just missing the caring and courageous people who are willing to help support and shape your life.

The people in your life who will look out for you. The trusted peers who can push you forward. The smart advisers who can accelerate your growth. The critical friends who can clarify your thinking. And the loving friends who will lend you a hand when you need one. People who can make your life a little easier.

Allies make things easier

If you have ever played a video game, you'll be familiar with the concept of power ups, the bonus items integrated into the game that give a player more strength, more power, a hidden secret or extra life to complete their quest.

If you sat down and played the game with a more experienced player, they'd share tips about these: 'Hey, be careful there is a trap right there. You won't be able to cross that river without a light. When you reach the dragon's den, make sure you take the second door.' The more experienced player is further along in the game, so has insights and experience that can help you advance. This is why allies are so advantageous.

Just as a more experienced player can help you find shortcuts, avoid obstacles and get through the video game, allies play this role for us in real life. If you are prepared to ask and willing to listen, allies can provide insights and wisdom to help you achieve some seemingly impossible task or give you the support you need during a difficult time.

Steve Jobs did this in 1985. When he was sacked from the company he helped create, he didn't sink into the shadows and resign himself to the setback. He turned to his allies to support his comeback: people like Bill Hewlett, Joanna Hoffman, Larry Ellison and Alvy Ray Smith, who had experienced and overcome corporate and creative adversity and could help him find a way back.

The allies you accumulate in your network will need to be diverse, but the ones you choose must have three important characteristics:

1. Honesty

It's nice to receive encouragement and praise, but there are times in life when you need more than just steadfast support. You need people who are brave enough to tell you the truth. Surrounding yourself with people who never disagree with you will limit your potential. A good ally is brave and will tell you the truth.

2. Respect

An ally you don't listen to is an acquaintance – someone you go to for advice but disregard because you don't respect their role, reputation or results. Finding someone who is more progressed than you, or even better than you, will ensure you are challenged, stretched and more likely to grow.

3. Trust

The baseline for any ally is that you trust they want to see you fulfil your potential and succeed. If the support you receive is predicated on that person being paid, is protecting the continuity of their contract or constantly reinforcing their own ideas or interests, everything falls apart.

Building a support network is something we don't invest in enough. The time and effort required to get a return on investment seems too long and too hard. Until of course we need it. Like insurance, we don't see the value of spending money to protect our home until the floodwaters start rising. Do you really want to be the helpless person sitting alone on the roof, praying for help to arrive?

Recruiting allies who give you sound advice not only helps you make good decisions, it prevents you from making bad ones. People who believe they are too smart, too senior or too complete to seek support are often the ones I see struggling the most. Usually to the detriment of their career, company and life.

If you feel like you have plateaued, lost your passion, feel isolated or are bordering on burnout, perhaps you need to recruit some allies.

Don't rely on Dumbledore

We sometimes struggle to build a network because we have a constrained view of who they should be. We observe popular culture and think one wise mentor – like Yoda, Mr Miyagi or Dumbledore – is all we need to support and guide us. But the reality is we need a broad network of people, with diverse skills and expertise, to support the various aspirations we have for our life.

To help you consider your current network and unearth some new people you could potentially recruit, there are three types of allies to consider:

1. Mates
2. Mentors
3. Masters

Mates are the people you connect with deeply, even if not regularly. They are the people who lift your spirits and keep you sane. The ones you invite around for a midweek pasta, glass of red and casual conversation. They're the friend at the end of the phone who will listen to your rant, then recalibrate your perspective. They're also the ones who know your intention to buy a convertible sportscar is a product of your ego, not good decision making, and will point that out to you. This is why our good mates can make great allies.

Mentors are the people who can help you achieve your aspirations and goals. Looking to leave your corporate job to start a scrapbooking business full-time? A business owner who is ten years down the track from you, experiencing a level of success you aspire to have, can teach you a lot. It doesn't matter if they have never run a scrapbooking business specifically, they've spent years gaining lessons and insights that can accelerate your success. Like how to find customers, market a product or reduce shipping costs. Mentors are not just for business either. You can also use mentors to get fit, become a better cook, learn a new language or set up your self-managed super fund. Ask a mentor smart questions and you'll get smart advice.

Masters have specific skills, expertise or experience you need to advance. These valuable people provide new ways of working, specialised skills or specific insights you cannot source on your own. Recognised as experts in their fields, these people may not be in your immediate network but create quality content you pay attention to in order to progress your personal and professional life. Like Adrian Salisbury, who I have never met but who played an important role in helping me create my member learning community, The Better Life Lab.

When developing your network, you need to do more than pay for a program or meet up once a month. You must also be vulnerable. If you turn up looking to protect yourself by proving you are capable, right or flawless, you will fail to progress. When allies get access to your life, they can ask the difficult questions you may not want to hear but which are critical to your personal and professional growth. This means opening yourself up to questions that can sometimes hurt, or make you initially dislike the people whose counsel you seek. Which is what happened when I met my mentor, Ted.

Early in my career I was attending an emerging leader program and was being observed as I participated in a team building exercise. I was asking good questions and assisting the group, but as it turns out, was not helping the team progress in the challenge. They were unsure and struggling to see a way through. I wasn't. I could see a way forward. But rather than take the lead, I was worried about coming across as bossy – and what people would think of me if I pushed my own ideas too hard. I asked too many questions rather than suggesting a direction. Ted, who observed me and was facilitating the program, asked in the debrief, 'Andrew, why do you have to be liked all the time?'

My first thought *wasn't*, 'Thanks, Ted, for that insightful question. I'm not exactly sure. Let me consider that.' My first thought was, 'I don't have to be liked. I share my opinions all the time. And why the hell are you picking on me? I was one of the people contributing.'

Over the course of the day, the penny dropped.

Ted wasn't criticising me. He was asking me to reflect on my leadership and level of contribution so I could make the most of my life. He was giving me a rare and generous gift. A gift I ended up valuing so deeply Ted became a long-time mentor and friend and one of the most influential people in my life.

Building your network

If you are an introvert reading this thinking you could never approach one person, let alone a network of them, fair enough. We can start with something easy. Think about one goal and focus on finding a master who can help you achieve that goal. You don't have to approach them, or meet face to face, but their online course, latest book or YouTube channel might help progress your aspiration.

If you are more willing and want to get started, we can do that too. While there is no one right way to recruit allies, there are five questions that will help you find the allies you need so you can live the life you want.

1. What do you want to achieve?

Deciding on a meaningful goal will help you define what support you need from your network. Are you starting a new role? Need a sounding board for decisions? Crave stimulating company and conversation? Or perhaps there is a particular skill you are trying to improve. The key idea is to understand what kind of support you need so you are discerning about who you approach to be an ally.

2. Who do you know that could help?

Effective allies are specific people who can help you progress your aspiration. Depending on your goal, this could be a peer, neighbour, previous leader you liked to work for or parent at your local school. Reaching out to people from different backgrounds, industries or stages of life will broaden your perspective, teach you new ways to do things and ensure your network serves you well.

3. How will you connect with them?

Approaching allies can be as casual, or formal, as you like. The key is to have an honest conversation about your aspirations. That way you can be clear about your intentions and expectations, and your potential ally can determine if they can meet them. If you approach a person that can't commit, thank them for their time and ask if you can revisit the opportunity at a future time.

4. How can you recognise their value?

A strong support network is a two-way street. You need to give back and can do this in one of two ways. First, thank them for the progress you make. If you receive a promotion after someone reads over your résumé, take them out for lunch to say thank you. The second way is to help *them* succeed. If someone in your network is looking for a restaurant to celebrate a special occasion, make a recommendation.

5. When will you know you are done?

Finally, you need to understand your goals are rarely linear or static. They will continually evolve throughout your career, experiences and life circumstances. As they do, reflect on your support network and, where necessary, recalibrate the people in it. Allies should always reflect the goals we are trying to achieve and raise the vibration of the life we are trying to lead.

Not every person needs the same kind of support. You might need a cheerleader. The person who believes in you because you are finding it hard to believe in yourself. While someone else might need a truth-teller. That special ally brave enough to name what you are avoiding. And someone else might need an expert. The person who has solved the specific problem they are facing.

The mistake most people make is recruiting the wrong type of ally for the wrong moment. You don't ask your cheerleader for hard feedback, or your truth-teller for encouragement when you are already doubting yourself. Get specific about what you actually need right now. Then recruit accordingly. Your network should be a toolkit, not a popularity contest. Giving your allies full access, and permission to ask provocative questions will enhance your life. The more access you give them the more helpful they will be.

Find your allies

Trying to make a meaningful contribution as you navigate the daily demands and pressures, can be an isolating, and anxiety filled experience. It doesn't have to be that way. Life gets easier, and a whole lot better, when you have a network of people who are willing to serve the promise you see inside yourself.

Recruiting some allies will help you learn how to show up more, cope better, and be more congruent and courageous in the way you live your life.

Obstacles become more manageable.

Success seems more achievable.

Life gets more enjoyable.

Go. Find your allies.

Insight ↷ Action

Premise

People who accomplish things rarely do everything themselves. The belief that you should do everything alone is costing you. It's costing you wisdom, perspective, resilience and the opportunity for growth; making the messy middle harder than it needs to be.

Practice

Identify one specific challenge you are facing and the people in your life who could offer some perspective on it. Not solve it for you, just think it through with you. Reach out to them and be specific about what you need. You'll be surprised how many people want to help when you actually ask.

Promise

You will experience the profound benefit of being heard and supported. More importantly, you will work out that the messy middle you are navigating does not require superhuman strength, it just requires some supportive allies.

Courage

Life shrinks or expands
in proportion to one's courage.

ANAIS NIN

Success without struggle is rare. Want a deeply connected and lifelong relationship? You are going to confront heartache and hurt. Want to chase that promotion or start your new business? You are going to experience fear *and* doubt. Want to win a premiership? You will have to embrace struggle and sacrifice. Want to apply some ideas from this book? You are going to feel uncomfortable and vulnerable.

The thing that stops us wrestling with struggle is fear.

Fear is the voice in your head telling you to protect yourself because you don't want to look bad. It's the voice that tells you to earn a stable income, not start your own business. It's your desire to feel capable rather than be curious. Fear is ignoring the mundane repetitions that help you perform under pressure. If you daydream about what you desire, procrastinating and putting things off until tomorrow, fear will ignore you. It rarely turns up when we are failing on our own.

But fear loathes courage.

Our willingness to do the hard work in the difficult moments. When we speak up. Connect ideas. Try something new. Find another gear. Talk back to our internal critic. Help a colleague. Fear has no power when we embrace opportunity. When we try, fail, learn and then try again because we choose to be brave in the face of fear. Just as a school bully backs down to anyone who stands their ground, we conquer fear though our courage to act.

The problem is, overcoming fear has been popularised as a simple rite of passage. The inspirational stories, both real and pretend, where the hero is called to action. They face impossible odds. Meet a series of enemies and overcome adversity. Then, in a final test, they summon all their strength to confront one final hurdle and prevail. The farm gets saved from the bank. The baseballers come to the field to play. The small business beats the big corporation. The despondent team eventually comes together to win the game. Success stories that happen over a one-minute musical montage.

But life isn't like that.

In real life, there is usually a messy middle.

Seeing someone step into fear and easily overcome the emotions they experience is misleading. It reinforces that struggle is easy and manageable. The reality is that most struggles are full of doubt, difficulty, heartache and hurt. Removing this reality reinforces the notion that struggle leads to success. We fall into the false belief that to overcome struggle, we just accept the grind, put in the reps and wipe the sweat from our brow, then emerge to save the day.

When courage is required, we expect to feel inspired.

But courage isn't like that.

Courage mostly makes us feel anxious and uncomfortable, so we try to avoid it. Courage makes us feel sick in the stomach and our legs to go weak. We lose sleep, doubt our capability and question what the hell we are doing. Courage is what speaks up when we are tempted to cut corners. Or when we lose patience with our partner and want to curl up and cry.

I wish I was speaking hypothetically, but I'm not. I'm describing my own experience in working to improve my marriage. Sarah and I met quite late in life. We were individually successful and had well established preferred patterns of behaviour. A strong one for me was relying on open communication to address relational problems. Sit down. Talk it through. Hug it out. Sarah's upbringing was different. Emotions, particularly the negative ones, were not something you delved into too deeply. When conflict occurred, the more I pushed for change, the more uncomfortable Sarah felt, and the more problems I seemed to create. You'd think, given my job, that I would have seen this pattern wasn't working much sooner.

Fear loved where my relationship was heading, so set up camp. It took me three years to find my courage. To accept what I was doing wasn't working, and a more connected and collaborative approach was required.

Eventually, one night I invited Sarah to sit down to have an open and honest conversation regarding our relational fatigue. We cried. Laughed. Argued. Questioned. Cried again. Eventually we agreed on some stuff. It was difficult. But that's the thing with courage. It rarely feels heroic when it's happening. It's messy and ugly and often hard.

But it's work worth doing.

Courage helps us accept the call to action to change our life for the better. It's how we bounce back from being fired. It's how we turn up to the first exercise class feeling frumpy. It's how we lead with vulnerability. And parent effectively. It's also how we break unhelpful patterns of behaviour and overcome hurt. As it turns out, it's also how you take a routine marriage and make it remarkable.

This section is an invitation for you to step into struggle.

To stand up to your fear, embrace courage and unlock the potential you've been hiding behind all these years. Because the only thing more exhausting than chasing a dream is running away from one.

If we are going to live life, we might as well live a good one.

This section will show you how.

9

Embrace

Embrace productive struggle

In April 1967 the Boston Marathon was an event steeped in tradition. An arduous test of endurance, it was predominantly considered a race for male athletes. Societal norms and unwritten rules, though not explicit prohibitions in the official rulebook, effectively barred women from participation. Kathrine Switzer, a young journalism student with a passion for running, was about to challenge the status quo.

Having trained rigorously and met the qualifying standards set by her coach, Arnie Briggs, she entered the race using her initials, K.V. Switzer. This was a common practice for her at the time – not an act of deliberate subterfuge. She was officially assigned bib number 261.

The early stages of the marathon unfolded without incident. However, near the 12-kilometre mark, the race director, Jock

Semple, a fervent guardian of the race's tradition and image, noticed Switzer was a woman. Incensed, he jumped off the back of the race truck aggressively accosted her, shouting, 'Get the hell out of my race and give me those numbers!' and attempting to physically remove her bib and force her from the course.

The shock, fear and humiliation of a direct and public confrontation could have easily justified Katherine withdrawing from the race. While her running partner Tom Miller intervened to block Semple, the defining action was Switzer's decision to keep running. As Switzer later recounted, the initial terror was potent and the thought of quitting surfaced. But it was swiftly superseded by a profound realisation: capitulating would reinforce the prevailing narrative that women were incapable or undeserving of such athletic endeavours.

The race was no longer about personal ambition.

It was about overcoming societal limitations.

Switzer ran with a transformed sense of purpose, each stride becoming a testament to her resolve. The harsh weather conditions and physical exhaustion were now filled with the significance of her defiance and perseverance.

She finished in approximately 4 hours and 20 minutes, not just as an athlete who had conquered the distance but as a trailblazer. Her refusal to yield in the face of overt hostility did more than secure her place in that race; it became a catalyst for a fundamental change in women's running.

You may not be trying to run a marathon, but maybe you have a work project that has hit a roadblock. Maybe you have a child with special needs – or are chasing a personal goal that seemed exciting at the start but now feels like an uphill battle. Making the decision to move your life forward usually comes with corresponding struggle. When that happens it's worth paying attention. The obstacle in front of you is teaching you how to get to where you want to go. It is showing you the way.

Battle bad guys

The work we want to get done always has a hard part. My son Benjamin is already learning this at an early age. Ben loves playing Minecraft and understands that to defeat the Ender Dragon and ultimately win the game, he must overcome Zombies, Skeletons, Creepers and Spiders. Bad guys that have been purposefully built into the game to prevent his progress.

Obstacles that hinder our progress are not just part of the gaming world – they occur in everyday life as well. Everyday bad guys can include an explosive temper, crippling self-doubt, unhelpful environments or even physical pain. They can be the negative people or interactions that make our life more difficult or demanding – and may even include past regret or negative emotions that zap your energy, focus or motivation. Our real-life bad guys can sometimes be hard to spot, so here are a few questions to help you identify some you may not be noticing:

- What are you avoiding?
- What bad habit do you want to break?
- What makes you feel guilty, sad or exposed?
- What do you want but are doing nothing about?
- What makes your day harder, longer or less enjoyable?
- What do people ask you to stop doing or modify?

Most of the time, the bad guys we experience are not horrible situations we must simply endure. They typically reflect some minor disadvantage or being stuck in less favourable conditions than we'd like. Or we're trying to do something that's difficult and feel overwhelmed or uncertain about how to progress. We are trying to get somewhere – but something is standing in our way.

Not every struggle we face is productive. Some just lead to anger and frustration. Knowing the difference is crucial.

Productive struggle stretches you beyond your current capabilities. The work is hard but doable with the right amount of effort. You can access the resources you need, and even if the path forward isn't clear you feel a sense of progress. Your effort is making things better. With unproductive struggle, situations and events are working against you, and no matter how hard you try you end up spinning your wheels and stagnating. It's frustrating and leaves you feeling dissatisfied. If you are not sure which struggle you are in, try this simple test.

Using a current struggle you are facing, can you think of three small ways your situation has improved? If you can, you are in productive territory. If not, it might be time to adjust your approach. You don't need to give up on your goal necessarily. You just need to find a better way.

Productive struggle may feel challenging, but the obstacles you are forced to overcome are not impeding your success. They are improving it. By making it harder to achieve our goals, obstacles help us develop skills and strategies that make us smarter, stronger and faster. These are valuable assets that enable us to move from where we are to where we want to be. But for this to happen, you must use adversity to your advantage. You must find the benefit and use it as fuel.

Recognising the challenge you face can be a powerful catalyst for purposeful growth. Think of the divorce that forces you to rediscover who you are, the career setback that leads to your true calling, the health scare that crystalises your life priorities. You discover a stronger, wiser version of yourself, because you are using the obstacle to evolve into who you can be.

It's easy to fool yourself into believing life is easier for other people, but not for you. That other people have better skills, more connections, greater motivation or abundant opportunities. Until of course you realise Jeff Bezos and Steve Jobs were raised by adoptive parents, Nelson Mandela changed the world from a prison cell and Missy Higgins struggled like many other singer songwriters but chose not to give up.

I don't have space to list the other famous, as well as less famous people, in a similar position to you, who also struggled and found ways to succeed.

People who took what should have held them back – what in fact might be holding you back this very second – and used it to move forward.

More than prevailing

How you choose to deal with discomfort and struggle determines far more than just whether you will prevail. It shapes *who* you become in the process. Think about the last obstacle you had to overcome. Did you think:

- 'This shouldn't be so hard.'
- 'Why is this happening to me?'
- 'Maybe I'm not as good as I thought.'
- 'Other people don't seem to struggle with this.'

Or were you asking:

- 'What can I learn from this?'
- 'What skills do I have to tackle this?'
- 'Who could help me navigate this more effectively?'
- 'What new skills might I develop from this opportunity?'

I suspect you identified more with the first set of questions, because the brain is wired to interpret struggle as a threat rather than an opportunity. This instinct served our ancestors well when facing predators but is less helpful for productive struggle. Consistently viewing obstacles through this lens reinforces a tendency to see problems rather than possibilities. You will probably get through most situations – but remain fundamentally the same on the other side.

Seeing obstacles through the second set of questions changes everything. Being curious results in new neural pathways being formed building stronger neural connections, much like how muscles grow stronger through resistance training. The struggle doesn't necessarily become any easier – but is *does* become more meaningful.

You are no longer just getting through it.

You are getting something from it.

You are building bravery that make future challenges less daunting. Building problem-solving skills that can be applied to other important areas of your life. And discovering strengths that enable you to confront situations you may have avoided in the past. You become someone who can work through difficult things. Someone who knows discomfort isn't necessarily a sign something is wrong – it can also be a signal you are taking on a challenge worthy of your potential.

Use the difficulty

In 2002 Sir Michael Caine was being interviewed by Michael Parkinson (yet to be knighted) in what could have easily been just another celebrity interview. But when Parkinson enquired about Caine's acting philosophy, the interview turned into a masterclass in how to turn adversity into advantage.

Caine shared a story from when he was taking classes as an aspiring actor. His American teacher asked him to perform a scene where he had to open a door while delivering his lines. 'There was just one problem.' Caine explained. 'The door was stuck, and I couldn't enter the scene. I was furious.' Instead of offering sympathy or suggesting something different, Caine's teacher offered three simple words that would change his approach to acting and life: *use the difficulty*. The teacher suggested rather than fight against the stuck door, Caine should incorporate the struggle into his performance. 'If it's a comedy, fall over it. If it's a drama, pick it up and smash it.'

Caine quickly understood the obstacle wasn't separate from the performance. It was an integral part of it, providing a level of realism that might have otherwise been missing. 'I took that approach and used it as a philosophy for life,' Caine said. 'Whenever difficulty arose in my life, I used it.'

The next time life presents you with a difficulty, you too have that choice. You can choose to fight against it, surrender to it or, as Sir Michael Caine did with the problematic chair, find a way to use it to your advantage. Here are seven practical strategies you can use straight away to make a start.

Stay composed. When we care deeply or aim high, stress and pressure come along for the ride. You can't afford to panic. Staying calm relies on you controlling your emotions rather than pretending they don't exist. Taking time to stop, breathe and direct your attention to what matters will help you manage stressful situations.

Find the opportunity. We decide what we will make of any situation. Far too often we react emotionally, get despondent and lose our perspective. All that does is turn a bad thing into a really bad thing. Find the opportunity within the obstacle and you will find a course of action that helps you progress.

Consider alternatives. We can create problems when we fight for the way we think things are *supposed* to be. Considering other alternatives without having to agree with them cuts obstacles and adversaries down to size.

Think clearly. Under pressure we lose track of what matters by worrying about the monsters under the bed. When you are feeling stuck, you need to think clearly. Plan your work. Break down goals into manageable tasks. Worry less about how to get it done – just do what needs to be done. The antidote for confusion is action.

Stride forward. Imposter syndrome and self-doubt are your allies; they are a sign you are stretching for something worthwhile. Believing the propaganda that they are bad will cause you to err on the side of safety and accomplish nothing. Instead, think of them as positive reinforcement and keep striding towards your goals.

Tolerate failure. There is a strong correlation between our ability to achieve great things and our tolerance of failure. Failures deliver breakthroughs if we are willing to learn. *What happened? What could be improved? What am I missing?*

These questions enable failure to show us the way – by showing us what isn't the way.

Practise persistence. If what you are doing isn't helping you progress, you should stop. For every other scenario, you should persist. Ask a follow-up question. Refine your idea. Knock on another door. Squeeze out another rep. Persisting in the face of adversity shows the obstacle, as well as your adversaries, that you won't be deterred.

Embracing productive struggle doesn't mean you can't take a minute to curse the gods and vent your frustration. Just don't spend too long taking stock. There are bad guys lurking around every corner, and to get to where you want to go you must be prepared to do battle with whatever is standing in your way.

This isn't about seeking out unnecessary hardship. Life will provide plenty of challenges without you looking for more. It's about approaching the inevitable difficulties with a mindset that turns them from obstacles to opportunities.

The ability to embrace struggle doesn't just help you overcome individual challenges. It strengthens every aspect of your life. It deepens your relationships and helps you become more comfortable with difficult conversations. It enhances your career and makes you more willing to take on challenges others avoid. And it clarifies your values and reveals what matters most to you.

The obstacle in front of you

We don't have much trouble accepting that work will often

involve physical labour, hard work or long periods of fatigue. We're not surprised when Mollie O'Callaghan trains hard in the pool or Ben Shewry spends hours in the kitchen perfecting a new dish before putting it on the menu at Attica.

But for some reason when it comes to investing that kind of effort into what *we* really want, we hesitate. We find ourselves stuck, because doing what we should be doing is a lot less enjoyable than doing something else. Checking your phone is easier than sitting with your thoughts. Racing from back-to-back meetings is easier than saying no. Blaming your spouse is easier than sharing how you really feel.

But if you do the work, you benefit.

You have to engage in struggle to get somewhere. And while I accept that you are unlikely to be competing at the next Olympics or serving saltwater crocodile at your next dinner party, you will have to overcome obstacles to achieve your ambitions. There will be situations holding you back or bad things happening that you need to handle. Moments when you can turn adversity into advantage.

There is always a countermove. A path that leads to higher ground and a more meaningful and enjoyable life. It won't necessarily be easy, and of course the work will be hard, but the path is there if you are willing to take it.

When something stands in your way, you can stare it down.

You can choose to embrace it and overcome it.

And you can emerge stronger and better.

Insight ⤳ Action

Premise

Not all struggles are created equal. Some stretch and teach you. Some just spin your wheels and keep you stuck. Knowing the difference is crucial to ensure you emerge stronger and better from the struggles you experience.

Practice

Think of something you're currently struggling with and ask yourself: Can I point to three ways this has improved in the last month? If you can, keep going. The difficulty is making you stronger, smarter and better. If not, the struggle isn't serving you and now is a good time to change your approach.

Promise

You develop the wisdom to know when to push and keep going and when to pivot and try a new approach. You will reduce your frustration and fatigue, stagnate less, and manage your way through the messy middle more effectively.

10

Bravery

Live (a little) scared

Ella Fitzgerald is a musical legend who inspired generations of musicians, from Frank Sinatra to Lady Gaga. Ella was a global sensation when she performed in Berlin in 1960. Her concert not only cemented her place as a music icon but offered a real-life masterclass in the power of failure. Known to shake things up from time to time, she decided to perform 'Mack the Knife' as a tribute to the crowd. The song had been written in Germany but taken back to America by Bobby Darrin, who turned it into a chart-topping success. The performance was going smoothly, Ella's voice filling the concert hall with the unmistakable warmth that made her famous. Then, about halfway through, with a further two minutes of the song to sing, Ella forgot the words. But instead of stopping or apologising, she started to freestyle. Improvising words, sounds and nonsense syllables, turning her mistake into a masterclass of musical creativity. The crowd loved it.

Later in the set, she showcased this spontaneous vocal artistry again while singing 'How High the Moon'. While her musicianship was already legendary, in forgetting the words to 'Mack the Knife' Ella introduced the world to scatting.

Her album *Ella in Berlin* won her a Grammy and showed that vocalists weren't just singers who recited lyrics but musicians capable of the same level of artistry as other members of the band. She created the pathway for vocalists to become artists. Forgetting the words helped Ella change the face of music.

We often avoid fear and failure, wrongly assuming it has an endpoint. That taking risks and embracing failure are acceptable on the way to success, but once we reach a certain level we should avoid doing so to protect the level of status or success we have attained. That being vulnerable or making a mistake in public would be a limiting move.

But the opposite is true.

As Ella showed in Berlin, taking risks, facing fear and being prepared to fail isn't something we stop doing when success arrives. It's critical to sustaining success. Confronting the areas of your life where you feel stuck is rarely simple, but the only thing more exhausting than chasing a dream is running away from one. It's time to step into your fear.

Two kinds of fear

We all experience a fear of failure. Whenever we decide to improve our life in some way, there is usually an element of risk. And wherever there is risk, there is also fear. The hard-wired cognitive bias that has kept us alive since the time we lived in caves.

In the Stone Age paying attention to fear alerted us to danger and kept us from becoming dinner. Today most of us don't have to deal with tigers anymore, but the fear emotion still runs deep. While it may feel the same, many of our modern-day fears are self-perpetuated, caused by our desire to uphold a level of social standing and status we have gained by working hard and fitting into society's narrow version of success.

We limit our possibilities when we mistake our self-perpetuated fears with our primal ones. They are not the same. A dog growling, baring its teeth and starting to run towards you on your afternoon walk is not the same as standing in front of an audience to give a speech.

In the first scenario, there is a real external threat. In the second, fear is triggered by an internal conflict. The threat is not an animal with teeth but feelings that bite.

Our fears make us uncomfortable, so naturally we prefer to play it safe. However, ignoring opportunities to tackle what is making you feel stuck is a recipe for an unhappy life. Behind every tired parent, lacklustre relationship, forgotten goal and plateaued career is a fear of failure. Past experiences we remember all too acutely that cause us to justify why we shouldn't commit to a forward course of action: the time we spoke up and were shut down, put in an application but got rejected, made a deep commitment but got hurt.

We rarely hold ourselves accountable for the countless times we have failed by inaction. The opportunities we didn't take, mistakes we made or current life circumstances we begrudgingly accept because we're not being bold enough. Accepting our inertia, unhappiness or missed opportunities is hard because, in doing so, we have to confront our fear of forward motion. That we are limiting ourselves by playing it safe to protect ourselves from failure.

But failure doesn't have to be fatal.

Confronting our fears sometimes makes us feel like Indiana Jones entering a dark cave of thick vines, deadly spiders and dangerous pitfalls. While it may appear scary and problematic, there is no need to panic.

Being brave is not that dramatic.

Stepping into what challenges or scares us doesn't have to happen in one gigantic leap. You can start with a small step to get your aspiration in motion. The longer you spend time avoiding fear, the more intimidating your fear becomes. Your perception about how hard, dangerous or scary things are grows proportionally to the amount of time you wait, overthink and delay.

Overcoming fear means coming to terms with the things that scare you. Reframing the emotion as an opportunity to take a risk, try something new and step outside your comfort zone. Knowing that in doing so you become wiser, stronger and a lot more likely to live a good life than those afraid to try.

Live (a little) scared

Forty-five years ago, on a family vacation to Canberra, I took Dad by surprise by declaring I wanted to jump off the 10-metre tower at the pool. I had been watching people leap off the platform all afternoon, and thought it looked easy. While energetic and full of life , I wasn't known for my acts of bravery. Eager to nurture this characteristic in his son, Dad took my hand and led me to a long line and large climb to the top of the tower.

As I waited my turn, I watched teenage boys in cut-off denim shorts leap off the tower with reckless abandon. When it was my turn, in what seemed like slow motion, Dad led me to the edge of the platform. The people waiting in the line behind me could see I was nervous and hadn't jumped before. Impatient teenagers offered me their questionable versions of encouragement to hurry up and jump.

Sensing my fear and the restless crowd behind us, Dad grabbed my hand and said, 'How about we do it together?' I nodded, took a deep breath, counted down from three, then jumped. I would prefer to tell you I wasn't scared, but the truth is I was shitting my shorts. We made the jump, and since then I've been leaping off metaphorical 10-metre towers my entire life.

The status quo is safer, but there is more to be gained from life by taking a calculated leap of faith. I wish I could say I never get nervous, never worry, panic or second guess myself, but that would be a lie.

The truth is, I just do it scared.

Fear is not the enemy. It's an invitation to grow.

A compelling life is rarely created in comfort. If you want to pursue better, you will sometimes need to operate at the edge of your confidence and level of experience. This can be debilitating if you reinforce what could go wrong. You cannot progress if you are unwilling to make some mistakes along the way. You need to become familiar with failure.

Take more photos

Shortly after Sarah and I got married, we met with our wedding photographer to go through the photos she had taken on the day. While we had the usual group family shots taken, we were more interested in seeing the images she captured of guests enjoying the celebration – the natural, unposed photos that would allow us to look back and really remember the day.

The pictures she took were amazing, so I asked her, 'Katie, how did you get so many good shots? These are brilliant.' 'Didn't you hear me clicking away?' she said. 'I took over 1200 photos.'

It made complete sense. We were seeing the best 150 pictures she had taken on the day. Not the entire collection.

Taking 150 brilliant wedding photos is a lot easier when you are prepared to take 1050 bad ones. The idea that taking more photos was the key to success has stuck with me ever since.

The media are full of mythical stories about overnight success. The reality, however, is that most success stories take a long time. The overnight success story is a result of producing a body of work over years. Shakespeare wrote 37 plays and 154 sonnets but is primarily known for a small number of classic pieces. Pablo Picasso produced over 17,800 works of art, of which only a fraction are noteworthy. And it took James Dyson fifteen years and 5216 prototypes to get his revolutionary bagless vacuum to work.

Where in your life could you take more photos?

Where might you find more health, happiness or joy by investing your time, energy and effort to build a body of work? Getting unstuck becomes surprisingly easy when you stop believing you have to be perfect. Pushing yourself to the edge and exposing yourself to your fear so you can become more alive, do work you're proud of and live a fulfilling life.

There is a valuable process for engaging in productive failure, but it must be applied individually to the situation you want to change. Whether you want to get better as a leader, public speaker, or build a life that better reflects how you ideally want to spend your time, you can follow this process to optimise your learning and progress.

1. Start smart

Choose the right environment to practise the skills necessary for you to succeed. Instead of pitching your project to the entire team, sound out a couple of key people including those prickly colleagues you believe will be disagreeable. That way, you can genuinely test your idea but also contain the damage if it doesn't land straight away. Finding the right level of risk to take will enable you to tolerate the discomfort of trying something new without your fear response hijacking the situation.

2. Find the sweet spot

Define your developmental sweet spot by choosing an action that's scary enough to be daunting but safe enough to be doable. Finding this balance will prevent you from attempting something so hard you avoid it or so safe you don't learn anything useful. Every time you practise, you carve out new neural pathways that allow your brain to stress less so you can better focus on the task at hand. This is where effort can be high and progress seem slow, so be kind to yourself. Remember, you can't go from the couch to 5k in one day. Whether you're building physical skills or mental ones, keep extending yourself over time by adding difficulty or the level of pressure. Constantly challenging your skills will generate a good pace of progress, mitigating the need for major leaps of faith.

3. Reflect and learn

Reflection matters, because insight without action will just make you a well-informed person who remains stuck. To get the most out of every effort you make, big or small, reflect on the experience with curiosity, not judgement. I like to use a strategy called 'Wow, First, Now and Next'. Wow involves capturing everything that went well that you want to take forward into the next experience. First means writing down all the reasons things didn't work out or go as you intended then crossing out all the factors that were outside your control; these are just unhelpful distractions. With Now, focus on what remains. These actions shape the Next path for further progress. The quicker you can apply your insights, the faster you'll make progress, and the less fear you will feel.

Embracing risk and failure vaccinates us against fear.

Just as introducing weak antigens stimulates our immune system to prevent further infection, exposure to productive failure builds our immunity to fear. Each dose builds our ability to cope with challenge, setbacks and struggle, allowing us to push boundaries, tackle thorny problems and write the clumsy first draft of your new book.

Seeking out opportunities we might find intimidating or uncomfortable isn't natural, but it is essential. Of course you are going to miss as often as you master, but your willingness to learn from failure directly correlates to the level of success you will experience in your life.

A playground for potential

Everything you want in life stands on the other side of fear. The relationship you've been longing for. The career that would fulfil you. The conversation that would heal old wounds. The project that keeps calling you. They are waiting for you, but the barrier standing between you and the life you desire, is fear. The prehistoric emotion impeding your potential.

Fear isn't your enemy.

It's your invitation to grow.

That tightness in your chest. The voice telling you to stay small. To play it safe and choose the familiar path. That's fear pointing you toward your next breakthrough. Showing exactly where your potential lies dormant and where your power is waiting to be reclaimed.

As soon as you choose to dance with fear rather than avoid it, you break the cycle that keeps you circling around the same problems, having the same conversations and settling for the same limited outcomes. You experience a profound shift where fear becomes a playground for your potential.

That's the entire point of this chapter.

To free you from a prison of sustained stuckness. To make a radical shift that finally enables you to break through a messy middle you have been bumping into for months or maybe even years. Because on the other side of every limiting fear you have lies your extraordinary life. Maybe it's time you chose to live it.

Insight ⤻ Action

Premise

We limit ourselves by playing it safe to protect ourselves from fear and failure. Waiting for it to disappear before you move forward is a mistake. It won't. Fear isn't the enemy. It's your invitation to grow.

Practice

Identify one thing that scares you. Ask yourself: what's the smallest version of this I could attempt? Not a giant leap. Just a small step. One that's scary enough to matter, but safe enough to take. Start there. Each small step you take while scared builds your immunity. The longer you wait, the bigger the fear grows.

Promise

When you step into fear you start chasing your dreams. You break the cycle that keeps you circling around the same people and problems keeping you stuck. You become wiser, stronger and more likely to succeed than those afraid to try.

11

Reflect

Pursue continual growth

In January 2017 I was sitting on my couch riveted to the TV as I watched Serena Williams beat her sister Venus, to win the women's singles tennis title. It was her seventh Australian Open title and her twenty-third major singles title. She surpassed Steffi Graf as the holder of most single major titles. By nearly every metric, Serena Williams was a modern-day superstar.

What many people didn't know about the greatest female tennis player of all time was her habit of keeping a meticulous diary. Her journal wasn't a notebook of random thoughts and fleeting emotions, it was a comprehensive manual for her own mastery. She documented obvious things, like her training regime, but also included detailed reflections about her opponents, specific cues for her serve, reminders about what to focus on in high-pressure points and crucial insights about how she prepares and performs. It was a deeply insightful resource she used to navigate the many messy middles she encountered during her professional tennis career.

Despite being a titan on the tennis court, Serena instinctively knew things were not always going to work out. She wasn't going to win every tournament. She wasn't going to finish every training session feeling ready to face her competition. Not every sponsor would want her endorsing their product, and she wouldn't feel like World Number One every single day she stepped out of bed.

The same is true for you.

Not everything you do is going to work out.

But unlike Serena, who pauses and takes time to reflect in order to equip herself when times get tough, what do we typically do when we find ourselves in the messy middle? For most of us, the instinct isn't to pause but to push harder. We double down, and work harder and longer, believing that's the best way to manage the messy middle we are in. This is why we feel stuck, even though we are working harder than ever. We are trapped not by a lack of effort, but by a lack of awareness.

How to become Oprah

Most of us move through our days with just enough awareness to keep functioning. Our regular bouts of stress, stuckness and failure are explained with simple, shorthand responses like

'I'm stressed', 'I'm just tired' or 'I feel overwhelmed'. While these labels may be accurate, they are derived for convenience due to a lack of deeper thinking and genuine understanding of our life experience. We are subconsciously choosing to overlook our blind spots and patterns of behaviour that are causing life to be dull, difficult or demanding.

When you stop questioning yourself, you stop discovering yourself, limiting the likelihood you will become all you are capable of being.

A mistake Oprah Winfrey almost made.

Long before she became an icon, Oprah Winfrey was a 22-year-old news anchor in Baltimore trying to forge her career as a broadcaster. As a black woman working in a cut-throat male-dominated industry, Oprah made the common mistake of trying to advance her career by being someone else. She let the station change her name to Suzie. She got a perm that made her hair fall out. When reporting on tragedies, she tried to remain detached and professional, like her idol Barbara Walters, when every instinct told her to connect and help.

Despite her efforts, Oprah's reputation slowly declined as she lost sight of who she was, trying to fit a mould that just wasn't her. Fortunately, like Serena, Oprah kept a journal, which she decided to read as a way to cut through the mental clutter and confusion she was experiencing in her career. This was the beginning of some deep and serious reflection. Reading page after page she started to see a pattern: the deep disconnect between the person in her journal and the person she was trying to be at work.

After eight months, her reflection boiled over into action. She stopped trying to be a perfect, detached anchor. She let her empathy show. She ad-libbed. She gave more of herself. The station managers were horrified. They told her she was 'too emotional' for the news and fired her as an anchor. But for Oprah, being fired wasn't a failure; it was a release. It was the world confirming what her own reflections had already told her: she was in the wrong role. She wanted to be authentic, even if that cost her the job she had thought she desperately wanted. The station moved her to a local talk show, and the moment she sat in that chair, it felt, in her words, 'like breathing'.

It was the breakthrough she needed.

She excelled as a talk-show host, catapulting her television career, shaping her reputation as an actress, author, television producer and media proprietor.

Oprah didn't become a superstar by getting a new job. She used the power of reflection to reclaim her awareness, which gave her the insight and courage to act and by doing so break the unhelpful pattern keeping her stuck.

Making time to reflect, with small adjustments along the way, adds layers of learning that help us better understand ourselves, the world around us and what it takes to succeed. Action and reflection are inseparable companions for living a good life. Without the courage to act, we would never move forward and progress. And without the willingness to reflect, we would never learn from mistakes and grow. We remain busy but not necessarily growing or changing the trajectory of our lives. This is the great paradox of struggle.

The thing we need most – a moment to pause, breathe and reflect – is the one thing our modern lives seem engineered to prevent. We treat reflection as a luxury. Something to do on our birthday, annual vacation or New Year's Eve – or when things have calmed down and we are less busy. But things rarely calm down on their own. The inbox never empties. The phone constantly pings. And the demands never stop.

So we remain stuck in unhelpful struggle, not because we're not good enough or working hard enough, but because we're not reflecting and learning enough.

Improvement isn't automatic

Most of us know that effort alone doesn't create growth. The boring team meeting, stressful commute or mediocre sex, done over and over the same way, will rarely improve. To achieve different results we need to take different actions, and this only happens when we successfully pair action and reflection.

Something we know, but very rarely do.

Take, for example, the last time something went wrong on a project at work. What was the feeling in the room? Was it a tense search for who to blame or was it an open, honest exploration of what could be learnt? Whether as part of a team or individually, for most of us the default is the former. We brace for impact, our defences go up and the opportunity for reflection and growth vanishes in a fog of fear and finger-pointing. This approach rarely leads to positive outcomes, and in high-stakes environments such as vascular surgery a culture of blame isn't just unhelpful, it's dangerous.

Which is why the Leiden University Medical Centre in the Netherlands decided to reinvent their team meetings to better mitigate risk and improve patient care. The team of vascular surgeons, residents and nurses instituted a practice of weekly reflective meetings. Meetings that didn't just focus on the complicated cases or the ones that ended in failure, but every case. They even discussed the scheduled surgeries for that week to anticipate challenges before they arose.

A simple shift that changed everything.

By depersonalising failure and making learning a collective responsibility, the meetings transformed from individual judgement to shared understanding. The focus moved from 'Whose fault was it?' to 'What can this teach us?' This created a space of psychological safety where team members felt empowered to speak up, to question assumptions and to share their insights and intuition about a patient without fear of reprisal.

The team developed a collective intuition, a common language for risk and a deeper, more nuanced understanding of what excellent care looked like in practice. They learnt to see the full spectrum of possibilities, not just the binary of success and failure. The goal was never to create a perfect, error-free system. It was about building a culture of reflective practice, which resulted in better communication, stronger collaboration and ultimately improved patient outcomes.

This is the true power of reflection.

There is little correlation between how fast you swim and how much energy you put into it. In fact, people who are drowning burn plenty of calories, but they don't go anywhere. When we are stuck or have to confront a new problem, putting in more of the same effort may not necessarily be the answer.

We may be better served building a regular reflection routine into our lives so we identify the subtle forces helping and hindering our progress and discover a more direct and fulfilling path to the things we are trying to achieve.

The 3R method

Understanding the power of reflection is one thing. Building a practice that feels authentic and executable, rather than another task on your to-do list, is another thing entirely. I use a powerful tool with clients to help them incorporate reflection into their everyday life, which you might find useful too. It is called the 3R method, which stands for Reflect, Recognise and Recalibrate, and uses three simple columns: a summary of the situation and what happened in the first column (Reflect), positive observations in the next column (Recognise), and suggestions about what could be changed or done differently in the last column (Recalibrate).

The 3R method is a practical tool that pairs action with reflection. You can certainly do this as a mental exercise, but I would recommend using pen and paper for the first few times.

Write the date at the top of your page and draw three columns. At the top of each column, write the headings or create a symbol that represents that word in your mind. Then complete each column relating to a specific conversation, interaction or period of time you want to reflect upon. The aim is to capture a snapshot of your thinking to strengthen your reflective practice.

1. Reflect

Write down what happened with honesty and without judgement. Think of yourself as a journalist reporting the facts from your specific situation. *What occurred? What conversations took place? What decisions were made, and what were the results?* Reflection means gathering the raw objective data without labelling it as good or bad. You might note that you had three client meetings, that a project deadline was missed, that a team member raised a concern or that you spent two hours on a task you had initially planned for one. This column is a neutral record of what happened and a critical foundation.

2. Recognise

Identify the decisions, actions or approaches that worked for you. *What was done well? What elements moved things forward or contributed to positive outcomes?* Perhaps you prepared thoroughly for a meeting and it showed in how smoothly it ran. Maybe you asked a clarifying question that prevented a misunderstanding. Or you stayed calm under pressure and that steadied your team. The Recognise column is about noticing the things you did, how you showed up and the choices you made that contributed to the results you want to see more of. These are the elements worth remembering and replicating. The patterns of success you can lean into again.

3. Recalibrate

Use your insights from the first two columns to shape your responses in this final column. This is where you ask yourself with honesty, *What would I do differently to get an even better outcome?* Your primary goal is to identify specific actions or choices that could have improved the situation. Perhaps you could have prepared differently, communicated more clearly, started earlier, asked for help or made a different decision. Only focus on what you could control and where your actions could have been more effective. These become your adjustments for next time. The small shifts that compound into meaningful change.

The 3R method is a simple way to pause, reflect and improve how you are living your life. This process can complement your existing journaling practice, be a viable alternative to the flawed New Year's resolutions you make each year or a targeted way to reflect on a personal goal or specific project with your team. *What happened? What worked? What would*

I change or do differently? By asking yourself these questions at a time and pace that works for your life, you learn about yourself and become more able to navigate the inevitable setbacks and struggles that lead to meaningful growth.

Make better mistakes

Taking time to reflect is a quiet power in a loud world. It's the deliberate pause that separates the master from the amateur, the resilient from the rigid and the engaged from the exhausted. It's the difference between accumulating experience and cultivating wisdom.

But this practice is not about naval-gazing, overthinking or dwelling on the past. It's about learning to make better mistakes. Because there are two kinds of mistakes in this world: the ones you learn from and the ones you repeat.

The first kind is a teacher.

The second is a cage.

Reflection is the key that unlocks the cage. It's the tool that allows you to see the game film of your life not as a critic but as a coach. To see the patterns you're running, the blind spots you're missing and the small adjustments that could change the outcome of the next play. It's how you stop being surprised by the same setback, frustrated by the same obstacle and trapped in the same loop.

Please don't treat reflection as a luxury you can't afford. Instead, treat it as the most essential, strategic and leveraged practice you have. It's the work that makes all the other work, work. It's the quiet engine of your growth. And it's the practice that ensures that no matter what happens in the messy middle, you are never just busy. You are always getting better.

Insight ⤳ Action

Premise

When things don't work out, our instinct isn't to pause and reflect but to push harder. When you stop questioning yourself, you stop discovering yourself, causing you to get stuck, not from a lack of effort but from a lack of awareness.

Practice

Improvement happens when we pair action with reflection. Over the course of the next week, try building a regular reflection practice into your daily routine. Take a walk, write in a journal or sit quietly with your own thoughts for ten minutes. As you do, ask yourself *What happened? What worked? What would I change or do differently?* to capture the valuable lessons from your day.

Promise

Each day will give you data for personal improvement. You will notice the blind spots and patterns of behaviour restricting your progress, giving you a more direct and fulfilling path to the things you are trying to achieve.

12

Progress

Make progress visible

In 1915 Claude Hopkins faced an impossible task. The legendary advertising executive, who had built his reputation selling beer and soap to millions, was facing his biggest challenge yet: convincing Americans to brush their teeth using a product called Pepsodent. Hopkins knew his greatest challenge wasn't that people weren't brushing their teeth. It was that Americans had *never* brushed their teeth. Fewer than 7 per cent of the population owned a toothbrush.

While many advertisers would focus on the health benefits, Hopkins spent weeks reading dental textbooks searching for something different. He eventually found his advertising angle in an obscure reference to 'mucin plaques', the thin film that naturally coats everyone's teeth. Hopkins' initial campaign asked people to run their tongue across their teeth to 'feel the film that makes your teeth look off and invites decay'. Americans became acutely aware of the film (that had always been there) and suddenly wanted it gone.

But Hopkins' real genius wasn't in identifying the problem. It was in engineering the solution.

Hopkins insisted two crucial additions be added to Pepsodent that no other cleaning paste had: mint and foam. The mint delivered an immediate burst of freshness that people could taste and feel. The foam bubbled and frothed, making the consumer's mouth come alive, showing them visible evidence of the toothpaste working. Of course both of these ingredients were theatre, a daily performance that showed people their progress in real time.

These weren't accidents. Hopkins understood that people needed to feel their transformation, not just believe in it. The mint told them they were fresh. The foam showed them they were clean. Together they created an experience so immediately satisfying that people began craving it.

The results were staggering. Three weeks after the first advertisements appeared, demand exploded. The company couldn't keep up with orders. Within three years, Pepsodent had gone international. Within a decade, toothbrushing had become a daily ritual for more than half of America, and Pepsodent was one of the world's best-selling toothpastes.

Hopkins had done something that seemed impossible. He'd taken a nation that had never brushed their teeth and made them unable to imagine starting their day without it.

Not through fear or shame, but by giving them something they could immediately taste, feel and see working. Claude Hopkins changed the habits of a nation by finding a way to give people a clear sense of progress.

The middle problem

Research has shown that most of us can identify when we feel stuck, and the pattern of how we get there is largely predictable. We start with lots of energy and typically finish with determination but lose our way in the middle, when progress is less visible and our motivation evaporates like morning mist.

It's easy to understand why we get stuck in the middle if you imagine lighting a candle in a pitch-black room without any windows. Lighting the first candle would create an immediate impact. Going from complete dark to light is substantial progress. The second candle would also have a big effect, albeit not as dramatic. Lighting the third candle would also be impressive, just not as impressive. These diminishing returns would continue until about the fifteenth candle, which would barely register on the brightness scale at all.

This is a core reason why the middle phase of our work is so problematic. We want our effort to have compounding benefits, not diminishing returns. We expect our effort to generate observable improvement, so results can be seen and momentum builds. But that's rarely how things go.

Much like the candles illuminating the room, making progress towards our goals is often the result of small, seemingly unnoticeable actions. Actions we often dismiss because we can't see any significant change for the effort we are making. For example, if we save a small amount of money each month, we still don't have a house deposit. If we go to the gym three times a week, we still may not be in shape. If we study Italian for an hour every Monday, we still haven't learnt the language. Despite our effort, we don't seem to be getting any closer to where we want to be.

The slow pace of change can be the catalyst for unhelpful actions that keep us stuck in a life we no longer want or enjoy. If you eat a chocolate muffin with your afternoon coffee, the scale doesn't move very much. If you work late at night and ignore your family, they still love you. If you procrastinate and put a conversation off until tomorrow, there will usually be time to have it later. These small decisions are easy to dismiss, but over time repeating such poor decisions and rationalising our unhelpful choices leads to a decline in our quality of life.

The middle is also problematic because misery loves company. When you are putting in effort but not seeing the results you expect, your inner critic turns up to remind you your results aren't good enough and you should quit. And what better way to discourage your effort than highlight your lack of progress?

This is the interesting thing about the messy middle. Doubt is loud and makes us feel like a failure, while progress happens quietly.

Think about the last time you learnt something new: a skill at work, a new hobby or even just figuring out a new app on your phone. Initially, you probably felt like you weren't getting anywhere. You were confused, making mistakes and felt frustrated. But if you chose to stick with it over time you worked out how to do it. You were in fact, making progress the entire time, but it wasn't visible until you reached a tipping point. This is equally true with your fitness, relationships, career growth and creative projects. In the midst of the messy middle, your brain is constantly building new connections, your body adapting and your skills are developing.

You just can't see it happening.

Your effort isn't being wasted.

It's just being invested.

Proximity to completion

Have you ever noticed you walk faster at the end of a bushwalk once you see the car park? Or that the last few minutes of a workout feel easier because you know it's almost over? That's your brain recognising proximity to completion. The closer you are to achieving your goal, the faster you move towards it.

In 1932 American academic Clark Hull discovered this phenomenon, which he called the goal gradient effect, by watching rats run through mazes. The closer the rats got to their food reward, the faster they ran. Decades later, researchers found the same pattern in humans. Students study harder as exams approach. Customers buy coffee more frequently to complete their loyalty card. And marathon runners speed up as soon as they see the finish line.

This is because our brain is wired to notice and reward progress. Even the smallest forward movement can be a powerful antidote when we feel stuck in our life. Your brain doesn't care if you climb Mount Everest or clean your desk drawer. It sees progress and releases feel-good chemicals either way.

When you are in the messy middle, progress is often invisible. You're doing the work but don't necessarily see the results. Your effort feels wasted so your motivation evaporates. This is when most people quit. But when you make progress visible – when you can see the small wins accumulating – everything changes. You realise you are not stuck. You are making progress. And that realisation is fuel you can use to your advantage.

You don't have to endure one seemingly long middle.

You can break a task down into lots of little ones.

Let's say you want to move from a job you loathe to one you love. A common sticking point for many people. You could break the process down into a series of smaller tasks. Writing a list of attributes you are seeking in your future role. Deciding on the location or salary level of the role. Commencing a search for suitable jobs based on your criteria. Assessing each role against that criteria, and deciding which roles are ultimately worth your application. These are smaller incremental steps you can take to find your future job.

Many of us chase the big win and completely overlook the small acts that reinforce a sense of progress. Then, when the goal takes too long, we get discouraged and give up, lamenting how our effort didn't amount to anything.

The truth is we are not designed to endure endless middles. We are wired for sprints and visible finish lines.

Understanding this psychological truth gives you a significant advantage over people who power through using willpower alone. That overwhelming career change becomes a series of manageable projects. Each completed task – whether updating your resumé or researching potential employers – triggers the same neurological reward that kept Hull's rats running faster through the maze. This isn't about tricking yourself or relying on motivation to get you through the messy middle. It's about recognising the positive impact progress has on your brain. Moving towards your goal naturally increases your energy. When you feel stuck, you rarely need more motivation. You just need to create the conditions where your brain stops seeing endless struggle – and starts to see achievable progress.

Make progress visible

We're not very good at paying attention to progress that is gradual or invisible. Petrol powered leaf blowers would be banned if the smoke they belched out was black instead of invisible. And fewer people would start smoking if the deposits on their lungs ended up on their face instead. On the other hand, Pinocchio had a hard time lying because every time he did his nose got bigger.

The idea is simple: if something matters, make it visible.

While we instinctively know we should measure our progress, most of us don't. We wear fitness trackers that can tell us the number of fictional floors we have climbed – or receive a badge for walking the equivalent of the breadth of Tasmania. But if someone asked us how we were measuring the progress in our life, all we would give them is a blank stare.

Here are nine ways you could make progress visible to achieve greater levels of success and satisfaction on your life.

1. Time invested

How many hours during the next month will you invest in the thing you want to do? If you spend 15 minutes a day for the next 30 days, that adds up to 7.5 hours. That might not seem like a lot, but when was the last time you took a whole workday to work on something you care about?

2. Date nights

Sarah and I go out five times a week and gaze into each other's eyes across the dinner table while the kids eat quietly. Not really, but we do schedule quality time together each month. Time spent with your spouse is time well invested. Keep track of the number of dates you go on.

3. Hours slept

Sleep is now recognised as one of the key contributors to high performance. You can track the quality of your sleep with a basic alarm clock, or for more specific data, a wearable device.

4. Financial health

You know that number in your savings account? That's a form of progress that tells you a lot about your financial health. So is the thickness of the credit card statement that gets sent to you every month. If yours is coming with a binder clip attached, see if you can work your way down to a single staple.

5. Quality connections

A lack of interaction with your friends, family or community can be an early warning sign for burnout. Tracking how many times you enjoyed the company of other people this month could save you from a serious breakdown.

6. Screentime

Maybe your goal is to reduce the doomscrolling habit you picked up during Covid. This one is simple. Apps (yes, I get the irony) like Bark and Freedom can track your screentime, or you can purchase a timed lockbox if your addiction needs a more serious intervention.

7. Level of stress

It can be equally interesting to track what you didn't do or what isn't going well. If you came home from work feeling irritable and stressed three nights last week, write that down. It can be a powerful reminder of the gap between who you are being and how you want to be living.

8. Healthy meals

Obsessing about exercise while ignoring what you eat is foolish. One of the keys to healthy living is meal planning. Tracking the number of healthy meals you made at home each week (or chose when dining out) can make sure you are on track with your diet as well as your deadlifts.

9. Personal growth

Maybe you want to develop your painting skills or a habit of gratitude. Have you booked into a class or sent a thank-you note to someone this month?

The best place to look for meaningful improvement is in the small things we consistently do each day. I've given you nine examples. The things you want to focus on will probably have their own unique form of progress you can measure. Pick one. Why just one? Because when it helps you, and it will, you'll want to measure progress in other important areas of your life.

Your temptation will be to overdo it.

Avoid that.

Your enthusiasm will discount doing just one thing and

encourage you to try and do six things instead. It's a trap. If you start small and reward progress, you'll end up achieving more than if you try and take on too much.

As a bonus, by reinforcing your progress you get to experience more enjoyment and satisfaction in the process. Choose one area of your life where you want to make meaningful progress and go make it happen.

Progress confidence

A lack of progress keeps you stuck.

It keeps you quiet.

It traps you on the couch.

It makes sure you never try.

It makes you believe you will never succeed.

Until you decide to embrace the power of progress.

If you make progress visible you don't just achieve your goals faster, you become the kind of person who rarely stays stuck. You stop fearing challenges, because you know how to break them down. You stop procrastinating, because you know small steps build motivation and momentum. You stop denying what matters, because you understand success is a series of small improvements.

You value the power of progress.

This isn't just a skill.

It's a superpower.

Go use it.

Insight ⤻ Action

Premise

When progress is low your motivation evaporates. But your big goals and most meaningful work take time. To sustain the effort they require, you need to make progress visible.

Practice

Choose an area of your life you want to progress. Make it visible in whatever ways works for you. A tally mark. A coin in a jar. A progress chart. Track your progress and watch it compound. When motivation is low, this visible proof will reinforce the effort you are investing isn't being wasted, it's being invested.

Promise

Seeing progress maintains your motivation and quietens the inner critic telling you to quit because nothing is changing. You stay the course, rarely stay stuck, and achieve the goals you set to build your better life.

Managing the middle

Real-life examples

This chapter looks at some messy middles my clients have found themselves in during the course of their day – from a busy human resource director to an overwhelmed parent – and how they applied the practices in this book to help them navigate their way through.

Embedded in each of these experiences are examples of how the practices are applied in real life. If you want to pursue better, you'll need to make these twelve practices a daily habit. Use the examples in this chapter as a guide to help you escape stuck, beat burnout and own your life.

Human resource director

Emma arrives at the office on Monday morning, opens her email and is met with a list of urgent issues that need her attention. An incident during Friday night drinks may have serious repercussions and there's a message to call her boss as soon as she gets in. Her weekend already feels like a distant memory.

Emma rings the CEO, James. He's heard about the issue on Friday and wants an update by mid-morning; and also wants a progress report on the company restructure Emma has been formulating behind the scenes. In the restructure a lot of people will change their jobs and some will lose them. James knows about Emma's plans but would like her to attend the board briefing this morning at 10:30 am in case there are any curly questions.

Emma agrees to attend, and as soon as she hangs up the phone realises, she has an existing commitment that clashes with the Board meeting. She has been working hard on a new leadership training program which starts today. Emma knows it's important for her to open the course and explain its importance to the business. She'll need to find a way to manage that clash.

Emma consciously finds **perspective** so she can focus on making some good decisions and manage the situation, rather than make it worse.

First, she focuses her attention on the positive impact she can make in each of the situations she has to manage by mid-morning. Emma immediately sees that she needs to handle two urgent matters – the Friday night drinks incident and the board meeting – and an important but not urgent issue, the leadership course. She uses the **transition with intention framework** to quickly decide she will handle each issue personally to reinforce her reputation in the business. She calls the two people involved to hear their accounts of what happened. She listens carefully and realises nothing untoward happened, neither party is concerned and no health and safety policies were broken. She adopts an activate strategy to make things better by scheduling a one-on-one catch-up with the senior leader overseeing the drinks on Friday to reinforce his role and responsibilities. Ten minutes – task completed.

Second, knowing the best way to support James is to alleviate the fears of the board regarding the restructure, Emma uses the **three reasons we fail framework** to show why the restructure is the right step for the organisation to take. She identifies the gap between the organisation's aspiration and reality and shares a clear five-point plan to close the gap. The presentation goes well, and James thanks her as she leaves. Fifteen minutes – task two is done.

Emma races directly to the leadership course, apologises for being slightly late and asks if she can address the group for five minutes. She explains her presentation to the board using **battle the bad guys** to reinforce the challenges facing the organisation and how the leadership program has been designed to equip leaders with the skills they to lead the organisation into the future. Emma feels good energy in the room: a willingness to step up and perform while acknowledging the work that needs to be done. Twenty minutes – her third task is done.

Back at her desk, Emma **reflects** on her day so far. The messiness of her morning was more personal than technical, but that's the nature of her job. She knows other **messy middles** will arise but feels **energised** by the way she managed the morning successfully.

School principal

Paul's morning just took a turn for the worse. The teacher's aide assigned to his class had to remove a student who was becoming agitated because they couldn't complete the work, and an already restless class has become impossible to settle. He now has a **difficult choice to make**: support the disruptive child who he knows is trying hard and making good progress – or placate a group of vocal parents lobbying to have the neurodivergent student attend a 'more appropriate' school due to the impact he is having on their children's learning.

His identity is being challenged and he worries about trying to appease two sets of parents, equally important stakeholders at his school. He's also feeling pressure about the staff meeting tonight to discuss brewing tensions around preparations for the school's major fundraiser. Distracted, Paul's class has become even more unruly, adding to the urgency he feels to bring everything under control. Paul realises he has gone quiet, lost in his own thoughts, and stopped communicating to the kids. Another challenging student is making her presence felt by yelling at someone for taking her seat. Paul wants to calmly get control of the class. Time for him to use some energy tools.

He's feeling overwhelmed, so takes thirty seconds to take a breath and quieten his racing mind. Paul moves his attention to a group of children that, despite the interruptions, are working well together. Paul **praises** the students for calmly continuing their work as a deliberate strategy to influence the rest of the class.

One simple action influences another group of students to get back on task, allowing Paul to go and talk to the yelling child and refocus her attention to the task they have been assigned. Feeling like momentum has shifted back in his favour, Paul uses the **uncomfortable truths framework** to quickly identify what he needs to do to get the class back to where he wants and needs them to be. Three clear and explicit instructions get that task done.

The teacher aide pokes his head back into the class to let Paul know that everything is under control with the table-turning child. He gives the aide a nod and returns his attention to the class and finishes off the lesson. After a quick visit to the staff room at morning tea to quell any gossip, he returns to his office and gets on the phone to speak with the table-turner's parents.

They initially react with a verbal outburst, but Paul remains **calm and composed** during their ventilation. Eventually the parents calm down, hear reason and express appreciation for the support and care Paul is offering their child. He then crafts a caring email to the remaining parents about the situation that occurred, how it was addressed and the steps taken to manage the situation and keep students safe. He realises parents may want to see him after school, but being proactive with his message helps him feel in control of the situation.

Despite a busy morning, Paul knows that as the principal of a small school there are still some twists and turns left in his day he will need to navigate. Sensing he is feeling a little fatigued from the morning, he calls a friend in his support network to say hello, share a laugh, and **renew his energy**.

Reflecting on his day, Paul realises the human element to his role is just as important as the educational one. Managing students, leading his team and liaising with parents can be stressful, and lead to a loss of enthusiasm for the job. Being a principal is demanding work, but practical tools enable him to navigate the **messy middles** and serve the school community well.

Elite sports coach

Damien's team has a crucial game this evening and his first task is to finalise selection. He hasn't slept well, procrastinating about the two final places on the team. He's still in two minds. Selection is a core task for a coach – but he sometimes finds himself flip-flopping between players, which is a major distraction from all the other things he needs to take care of.

Damien decides to **accept reality** and starts the timer on his mobile phone. He's narrowed his selection down to two players for each position. He starts with the most contentious decision, uses the elevate and activate decision-making process to make his final decision. Then he repeats the same process for the second position, and at the end of the fifteen minutes his team selection is complete. The task of actually writing down the two names releases some tension and he acknowledges the shift in his **energy**. Task done.

His next task is to use the **add value strategy** to plan the talk he'll give the team before they travel to the game this afternoon. The mindset he wants is controlled aggression. The game is a long-standing rivalry, so they need to play hard but impulsive actions have been costly the last two weeks. Damien wants every player to know their role and play with drive and determination, not rash emotion. He forms a clear plan, reinforcing the messaging from the week's training. He writes his key points on the whiteboard. Task completed.

Next, Damien makes a few calls to check last minute issues with support staff and it looks as though there is a problem. One player has reported in sick. Damien uses **perspective** to manage the situation quickly and effectively, to maintain his focus and feeling of calm. Satisfied everything and everyone is ready, he heads to the team gym for his usual pre-game exercise routine, which will energise his body and clear his head.

In the lead-up to the game Damien finds a quiet place to complete his preparation. He reads over his game plan so that he has every expected player and scenario covered, just in case. Five minutes before everyone gathers for the final briefing, he looks around the room and sees a purposeful hive of activity and quietly appreciates the level of capability and professionalism he has around him to **support** what has been a successful season so far.

During the match there's the usual combination of anticipated issues and unexpected drama. The opposition gets a jump on the team early and a key player gets injured before half-time. Damien is able to adapt and **evolve** based on his scenario planning before the game. In the break, he speaks to the team calmly, highlighting areas that require improvement to turn the game around.

In the second half the team returns to their game plan, and although the opposition responds with four goals of their own they gradually get on top and end up being ahead by two goals at the end of the game. There is an emotional response from players, staff and fans. Damien **takes some quiet time** in the review room to quell his own emotions before speaking with the players. He lets the players know he appreciates the effort they have invested and tells them to go and enjoy this moment with their friends and family.

By the time he gets home, he's tired but nowhere near ready for sleep. He's still emotionally digesting the evening's events and needs time to rest and **rejuvenate** before fulfilling his media commitments tomorrow morning. He reverts to reading a book as it allows him to quickly transition from navigating the endless **messy middles** that occur as a professional coach. Within half an hour, he's asleep.

Busy parent

Lisa's sole focus is just getting through her day.

She works flexible hours at a mid-tier accounting firm, and her job is unstable after the owner announced he was retiring and selling the business. She has no partner at home to share the load; she has financial worries to the point where money gets tight towards the end of the month; and she has no time or energy left at the end of the day to invest in exercising or socialising or pursuing interests of her own.

Lisa feels angry about her situation and guilty about not providing for the people she loves. Her children seem to be making some poor choices that may potentially limit them later on – all because she's unable to give them the stability and guidance they need and deserve. She's stuck in survival mode.

She feels rundown and worries about burning out wondering how can she keep going day after day.

It's mid-morning at work and already she's at the end of her tether. Her manager, Jason, has demanded that she prioritise an unexpected task. A high-profile client wants some advice on their trust account structure to make an important financial decision in the next forty-eight hours, but Lisa knows compiling the information accurately, will take longer than that. Jason has delegated the work to Lisa suggesting she call the client to extend the timeframe if she can't get it done on time. Jason should be the one making the call, but as usual, hasn't helped by taking work off her plate or relaxing timelines on her other projects. Lisa can feel the tension creeping into her shoulders and jaw. A warning sign she has learnt to listen to that tells her she needs to **embrace** the struggle and **stay composed**. Now is not the time for her emotions to get the better of her. She walks to a coffee shop close to the office, using the time to pause, find some calm and direct her attention to what matters. This allows her to accept the inadequacies of her boss and, as she teaches her kids, reinforce that she can **choose her response**. There's no point losing control and making the situation worse. Lisa uses the **transition with intention** to make a plan while walking back to the office.

She spends thirty minutes assembling the information and planning her conversation with the client, then dives straight in to picking up the phone. The customer is angry the firm cannot complete his request, but Lisa empathises, explaining meeting the deadline may mean inaccuracies in the information, putting the client at risk. When she believes the client is ready, she suggests providing an initial high-level overview, followed up by the full documentation by the start of the following week. The customer realises Lisa is trying to help and accommodate a difficult request, so ends the call sounding happy enough. Not perfect, but a satisfactory outcome under the circumstances.

After lunch she initiates a meeting with Sam, a colleague in the sales team, to discuss an idea she believes could **add value** to the firm's client management system. Sam likes her idea and suggests the two of them work together to create a plan and present to the partners' meeting next month. Lisa is excited. This could be the opportunity for the lateral career move she has been craving.

At the end of the work day she **reflects** on the way home, feeling satisfied that she turned around the challenging start to the day. Unfortunately, as soon as she walks in the door, it's complaint central. Her daughter Laura is complaining about one of her teachers, and her son Angus is complaining about his soccer coach. She feels the urge to tell them to stop, but knows lecturing them will do more harm than good. Some **support** is needed.

Angus seems more in need, so she starts with him. Using the **ask powerful questions technique**, she listens carefully and asks Angus a series of questions that helps reduce his anger and find some **perspective** to the issue he is facing. She repeats the process with Laura, helping her deal with her volatile emotions about a test that didn't go very well.

On the back of recognising her conscious **choice to connect** with her children, a powerful insight presents itself: although she cannot provide as much as some parents *materially*, she is developing her children's *emotional* strength in a way others struggle to match. Dealing with pressure and having to think clearly in emotional situations helped her today, and passing this gift on to her children will help them face adversity to.

As she thinks about this, she connects strongly with her **identity** as a single parent working through adversity and the strength she shows every day. Navigating life's **messy middles** with **resilience** and dignity sends a powerful message to the people who matter most.

She deeply appreciates who she is and what she does.

Conclusion

Barack Obama was about to lose control of the room. The president had been confidently delivering his immigration reform speech in San Francisco when an unexpected voice cut through the crowd. A young man – positioned just behind Obama as part of the human backdrop that adorns every presidential appearance – had broken the unwritten rule of silence. 'You have the power to stop deportations!' chanted Ju Hong, a 24-year-old Berkeley graduate whose desperation finally overwhelmed his restraint.

The Secret Service agents tensed.

Staffers exchanged alarmed glances.

The audience held its collective breath.

In that brief moment, what could have been an obstacle to Obama's message became an opportunity he never anticipated.

Most politicians would have seen the interruption as a barrier to overcome. Something to push past or silence. Easy for a president to ignore with a dismissive wave and subtle nod to his security detail, before returning to the teleprompter.

Instead, Obama turned to face his critic directly.

'Actually, I don't,' Obama responded, his voice carrying an edge of irritation that seldom broke through his composed exterior. 'And that's why we're here.'

The crowd stirred uncomfortably as the president engaged with the young activist. Hong continued his protest, his words carrying the weight of countless families torn apart by deportations. Obama raised his hand, not to silence but to use the moment to demonstrate, rather than just describe, the very challenge he was addressing.

'The easy way out would be to yell and pretend like I can do something by violating our laws,' Obama said, his eyes locking onto Hong's. 'What I'm proposing is the harder path. Which is to use our democratic processes to achieve the same goal that you want to achieve. It won't be as easy as just shouting,' Obama continued. 'It requires lobbying to get it done.'

Embracing the interruption meant the heckler didn't diminish the president's message but enhanced it. Obama demonstrated that the path forward isn't found by avoiding obstacles. It's found in the courageous act of embracing them.

You may not be running for president, but every day you too are presented with decisions that shape who you become. Metaphorical forks in the road where you have a choice.

You can stay comfortable or you can step into growth. You can stay quiet or you can stand for something. You can make an excuse or you can make an effort. You can wait until you feel ready or you can take a risk.

Every choice point is an opportunity to move forward towards the person you want to be. The more you align your aspirations and actions, the more comfortable you become with who you are. Life remains a work in progress but being congruent in the life you are living enables your decisions to come from a place of conviction rather than social acceptance or approval.

How content are you with your life right now?

I don't mean this as a surface-level question but as a much deeper one. Does life feel fine? Could you easily keep doing things the way they are – paying the bills, advancing your career, squeezing in time for family, friends and weekend sport – and still feel like you are living a good enough life? Or is there something lurking underneath that fine-ness. A subtle or nagging tension that better is possible?

Our tensions reveal deeper truths.

Truths that get ignored by busy brains.

We feel the tension in quiet moments when we compare our life to the one we imagined, or lying in bed at night wondering if we are settling for less than we can be. Then we push it away. We make ourselves busy and get distracted, convincing ourselves that everything is okay.

But it's not okay. Not for you.

That's why you picked up this book.

You want something better. A better career, better relationship, better health or a better life that feels more aligned to who you want to be. That deep desire calling you isn't arrogance or dissatisfaction. It's an unpretentious invitation for you to be who you really want to be. A wake-up call that's worth answering.

But this is where most people get stuck.

They read about it, see the value in it and even feel motivated to act upon it, but then life resumes and bounces back to normal. The demands keep coming, the challenges seem overwhelming and the internal chatter keeps chirping. And sooner than anyone would like to admit, they find themselves back in the same situations and behaviours they were trying to escape.

But you don't have to be one of them.

You can make a start. Not perfectly, when you feel ready or when you have it all figured out. You can start *now* by picking one practice from this book that resonates with you. Then take one small step that gets you started. One step that compounds and builds momentum, transforming you from someone who wanted to build a better future, to someone who did. You already know how to do hard things. You've navigated difficulty before and kept moving when it would have been easier to stop.

The capability exists in you.

It's just waiting for you to use it.

But – and this is a big but, because I cannot lie – it's on you. If you want your life to change, you have to change first.

You have to use the Better Life Index™ to develop your character, capability and courage, because there are going to be moments when you find yourself in the messy middle. Moments when you are bone tired and craving rest. When progress feels invisible. Or when you question if you're on the right path. That's normal. Being in the messy middle is how you know you're on a path worth taking.

When that happens, come back to this book. Return to the practices and let who you are and what matters to you be the psychological keel that keeps you steady. The more you do so, the more you learn to navigate life's most challenging moments with the most powerful tool of all. Your full self.

Start

A better future favours those
who dare to do things differently.

LATIN PROVERB

You know life doesn't always go according to plan. Some days you're flying and some days you're face down on the floor. That's the messy middle. You can't always see trouble coming, but with the right tools you can always turn it into something.

For the past eighteen years I've been helping individuals, teams and organisations transform stuckness into strength. If you are done faffing about and want to forge a new path forward, the next three pages give you great alternatives to turn insight into action.

Elevate your life

Now you know the messy middle exists, learn how to master it with this online course. Highly practical, you pick one area of your life calling for change, then apply the practices in this book to make that change. For less than the cost of your daily coffee, you'll make progress, build confidence and elevate your life.

andrewhorsfield.com/course

Strengthen leadership

Leaders must constantly manage challenge, change, and complexity. Some thrive on it. Others get stuck, burn out or disengage. If you are building something that matters, you know which kind you need. If your leaders could benefit from strengthening the skills detailed in this book, let's start a conversation.

andrewhorsfield.com/consulting

Make life better

Right now, people across different industries and life stages are coming together to connect, interact, and be inspired. The purpose of this community isn't fame, fortune or more followers. We come together to make our lives better. If that's also important to you, it helps if you have company. Come and join us.

andrewhorsfield.com/community

“You don’t have to be great to start, but you do have to start to be great.”

ZIG ZIGLAR

Acknowledgements

Writing a book is one of the hardest messy middles to navigate. This book would have fallen short of my aspiration without the honesty, dedication and care of some valuable allies. People who helped me when I got stuck, offered support and enriched every page of this book.

To my incredible wife Sarah: thank you for being patient during the longest book writing process I have ever known. Your wise counsel and constant support turned my ideas into a book worth reading. You read every word, edited chapters with care and clarified my ideas when fear, doubt or tiredness sabotaged them. I could never have done this without you.

Ben and Isabelle, you're too young to know, but your energy, love and curiosity fuelled my writing and influenced many of the ideas in this book. I hope these lessons find you when you need them most.

My deepest gratitude goes to Tony Sheppard. Thank you for believing in me and giving me your time, expertise and unwavering honesty. While our writing sessions were invaluable, they pale into insignificance compared to my enjoyment of our meandering conversations and building a friendship that extends well beyond chapter content and sentence structure. I can't wait to watch some cricket with you in the West Indies.

To my family: you continually help me navigate the messy middles in my life. Whether through robust challenge or resolute support, you help me find clarity and believe that anything is possible. Time with you makes me better. I love you all.

I am indebted to Kirstie Innes-Will for being a caring and considerate editor. Your enthusiasm and expertise made my words more economical and meaningful. A true gift. Duncan Blachford, you turned words on a page into art and entertained my pedantic nature regarding spacing, iconography and presentation. Thank you both.

To the brave souls who read early chapters and offered invaluable feedback. To Lisa Alexander, Julien Weiner, Dan Gregory, Shane McCurry, Jodie Wellman, Will Carr, Paul Roos, Wayne Taynton, Marc Champagne, Lucy McCullagh and Clint Hillas. Thank you. You made this book better.

This book also wouldn't exist without clients willing to road test and refine these ideas. Specifically, Rohan Davidson, Caden Hart, Gehan Davids, Julia Lawrence, Susan Evans, Vanessa Bishop, Dean Jamieson, Tim Cox, Nuwan Dishan and members of the Better Life Lab community.

And finally, thanks to you. The leaders, coaches, parents, principals and entrepreneurs working to achieve better. The path is full of potholes, but that's what makes the work worthwhile. Never stop pursuing what you care about, stepping into challenge and chasing your dreams.

Index

Andrew Horsfield is an author, coach and consultant. Over the past two decades, he has helped leaders in business, education, and elite level sport, tackle the challenges of human performance. He is the host of *The Messy Middle* podcast and creator of the learning community the Better Life Lab. He lives in Melbourne with his wife and two children.

andrewhorsfield.com